# Stencil Girl

## MIXED-MEDIA TECHNIQUES

*for* **MAKING** *and* **USING STENCILS**

*mary beth* **SHAW**

**NORTH LIGHT BOOKS**
CINCINNATI, OHIO
www.artistsnetwork.com

# CONTENTS

STENCIL THIS!                          4
STENCIL STUFF (SUPPLIES)               6

## Stencil Art

Think-Outside-the-Stencil Painting     10

Woulda Coulda Burn Wood                18

Unmask That Paper Doll                 22

Magazine Magic                         30

How Can You Resist a Fish?             34

Let's Get Dimensional                  38

Wax and Waning Encaustic               44

## Stencil Décor

Can-Can Lantern                        56

Felt-A-Rama                            62

Spray It Again, Sam                    66

Quilt Me Batik                         72

Improv Place Mat                       78

Hands on the Wall Wallpaper            82

# Stencil Fun

Painted Memories Travel Journal    88

All That Glitters    96

Eat Cake    102

T-ease Me    106

Greetings, Greetings, Greetings    110

**CONTRIBUTORS**    118

**RESOURCES**    124

**INDEX**    125

**DEDICATION AND ACKNOWLEDGMENTS**    126

**ABOUT MARY BETH**    127

4

# STENCIL THIS!

*I am a girl who loves stencils. As an artist, I know stencils have the ability to really make us look good. Stencils add beautifully complex detail to our art—easy repeats, dynamic silhouettes and layer after layer of glorious patterns. Oh, be still my heart.*

Stencils are undoubtedly one of the most versatile tools available to the mixed-media world, yet I am frequently asked how to use a stencil. I suspect people ask this question because there isn't really one straight answer. I mean, think about it. Some of the most frequent ways we see stencil art is in the form of graffiti—on railroad cars and in urban landscapes—on T-shirts or as tattoos. Mixed-media artists might wonder what stencils could offer for their art.

Well, I am here to tell you that stencils can offer quite a bit. They can be used with paint, pencil, marker, glitter and pigment; on fabric, paper, canvas, wood or clay; in fine art applications, on greeting cards or in journals—just to name a few applications. You can buy stencils, you can make stencils, and you can invent stencil effects with found objects. You can also use reverse stencils, which we call masks.

You see, because of their flexibility, stencils can be used so many ways that it's difficult to offer a quick answer about how to use a stencil. I am hopeful that this book will enlighten you about some of the ways that stencils can be used in your own work. And I will say right up front that I suspect I have only scratched the surface; in fact, I am pretty sure of it because I continue to think of more and more ideas each day. And the work provided by my contributing artists inspires me even further!

Whether you are a beginning stencil artist or an old pro, this book will offer you some fresh ideas to expand usage of your stencil library. Use this book as a starting point. You can flip through randomly and pick a project that appeals to you. Or read it from cover to cover. Look at the pictures and put on your thinking cap. It is my intent to provide you with inspiration that will spark even more ideas and propel you off into new directions.

Go see what you can do; surprise yourself, surprise me! I want this book to be the start of a continuing conversation. I have set up a site (www.stencil girlbook.com) for ongoing discussions. Come join the fun and share your ideas, photos of projects and any and everything stencil related. There is absolutely nothing I love more than talking about stencils and ways to use them. And I truly look forward to hearing from you.

Now you see why they call me Stencil Girl.

# STENCIL STUFF (SUPPLIES)

Stencil supplies can be as complicated (or simple) as you want to make them. Seriously. You can most likely find improvisational "stencils" around your house and use them with paints and sprays that you already own. Or you could go out and buy new supplies—and we all know that is a lot of fun, too. When looking at general stenciling supplies, there are four basic areas for you to consider.

## APPLICATORS

The main key to application is to keep it dry. Use as little paint as possible and you will get a cleaner result. Think dry-brush. With respect to the applicators themselves, many different items may be used quite successfully. There are brushes made especially for stencil usage. They come in different sizes and are quite nice. There are also brushes called scruffy brushes that are made for decorative painting. They work well with stencils, too. You can use inexpensive foam brushes, foam rollers, cosmetic sponges, a palette knife, an old credit card or, sometimes, even your fingers.

I had this idea that I was going to invent the perfect stencil applicator. That was until I found the sponge daubers manufactured by Tsukineko. They're made from a very dense foam that is highly absorbent so you can easily maintain a dry-ish surface. You can use them with paint, stamp pads, ink, whatever. They come in several sizes, including one that is so small it fits over your finger. If you use them with a gentle stroke or pounce, you can get super-clean stencil results. Plus, they clean up great and are long lasting. Like I said, I couldn't have invented anything better.

## SUBSTRATES

*Substrate* is a fancy word for surface. By surface, I mean whatever you are going to stencil on. And it could literally be anything—a wall, wood, canvas, paper, clay, fabric, glass. As you move through this book you will see that I have included ideas and projects for all of these substrates. It is my hope that this book will simply provide a jumping-off point for your stencil adventures. Once you get going, you will find yourself reaching for stencils more or less every time you work in mixed media. At least, that's what I do.

## PRODUCT IDEAS TO USE WITH STENCILS

acrylic paint  *  spray paint  *  latex paint
pens  *  watercolor paint  *  oil paint
gouache  *  airbrush  *  pencil  *  marker
water-soluble pencils and markers
spray inks  *  chalk  *  texture medium
powders  *  PanPastels  *  glitter
flocking  *  thread  *  wool roving
fabric paint  *  encaustic paint
Mr. Clean Magic Eraser  *  rusting compound
etching fluid  *  stamp pads
bingo daubers  *  rubbing wax  *  crayons
frisket  *  tempera paint  *  oil pastel
bleach pen  *  fondant  *  icing
spray icing

*I think you get the idea.*

## STENCILS

Available online and in art and craft stores, stencils—are often made of plastic, but Mylar is much more durable and tolerates heated applications. Some are made of oil board.

**Hand-cut stencils** may be torn or cut. You can make them using E-Z Cut Stencil Material, acetate, contact paper or scrap paper.

**Found objects**—anything with holes in it—can act as stencils: the side of a laundry basket, lace, doilies, plastic mesh, produce bags, screens, sequin waste, die-cut scrapbooking papers or templates for drafting.

**Masks** can be hand-cut from the same materials you use for stencils. Also consider chipboard parts, the edges of decorative scrapbook paper or drop-out parts from large stencils.

# STENCIL ART

*As a professional artist specializing in mixed media, I consider stencils one of my most valued tools. When I work in the studio, I keep them close at hand so I can easily grab one and add an element to my work.*

I rely on them to help me create interesting backgrounds, to integrate background and foreground in my paintings and to add otherwise intriguing effects to my work. I like the idea of surprise—where I put something in a painting and the viewer can't figure out exactly how I did what I did!

I have found that the more I use stencils, the more I love them. I am continually discovering ideas that had previously been unknown to me. Stencils kind of get under your skin—in a good way! I feel sure that as you explore their usage, you will also realize a lot more ways you could use them in your own art. Let's get started on a myriad of artistic applications!

# Think-Outside-the-Stencil Painting

Sometimes more is more. At first blush, this might appear to be one of those projects where you throw everything but the kitchen sink at the piece to see what sticks. But I am talking about *more* in the very best sense of the word, where one layer goes over the top of another to create something more complex and distinctly new; where edges and parts peek out from underneath one another; and where the texture and carving live happily ever after.

The idea is to use a geometric stencil to create a mixed-media piece. Use the stencil as your main composition guide. You don't have to add every single layer or use every single product like I did. The object is to think outside the stencil. Use your stencil as a composition tool, a painting pattern or an embellishment template. And then turn it and use it again and again. Repetition works to your advantage, and yes, sometimes more is indeed more.

## Here's a Tip

An offset palette knife is one where the blade touches the surface, but the handle is offset so your hand remains away from the surface and doesn't inadvertently smear your work. This type of palette knife is great as a small trowel, plus it has the flexibility for scraping and mixing. If you have a budget for only one palette knife, this is the one.

## WHAT YOU NEED

- *Claybord*
- *craft knife or carving tool*
- *geometric stencils*
- *detail stencil*
- *Wood Icing or texture medium*
- *palette knife*
- *baby wipes*
- *sandpaper*
- *acrylic paint*
- *paintbrushes*
- *Copic airbrush*
- *Copic marker*
- *paper towels*
- *glue*
- *mica flakes*
- *Derwent Inktense black pencil*
- *dimensional embellishment*
- *Scribbles Dimensional Fabric Paint*

1 Begin with a Claybord substrate. Carve into the surface with a craft knife or carving tool, using geometric stencils as a guide.

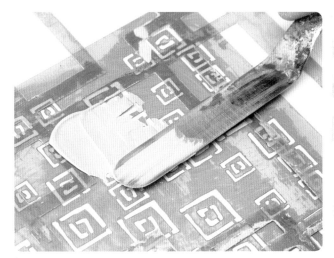

2 Add another more detailed stencil under the original stencil. Put a thin layer of Wood Icing (about as thick as the stencil itself) on the area covered by both stencils, using an offset palette knife. (See tip above.)

## Here's a Tip

When working in my home studio, I keep a dishpan of water nearby and drop my paint-stained stencils into it immediately after using. But a baby wipe makes cleaning stencils easy and is especially nice for removing gunky products you don't want to go down your sink, such as texture paste or Wood Icing.

**3** Remove the stencils immediately.

**4** Put the original stencil back on the substrate. Add Wood Icing in other areas of the original stencil, working around the area where you just put icing down.

**5** Add extra texture around the edges with the icing, using the palette knife. Leave some spots untextured. Let the icing dry completely. If the icing feels cool to the touch, it's not dry yet.

**6** Lightly sand the surface to remove any unevenness or sharp "crumbs."

**7** Choose two complimentary acrylic paint colors. (I'm using Burnt Sienna and Ultramarine Blue.) Blend both colors with a bit of white to make a beautiful gray.

8 Add a layer of paint wherever you'd like. Get enough on the board to lightly cover the whole thing.

9 Rub paint into the crevices of the texture using your fingers. Add more paint in layers as desired until your composition pleases you.

10 Drybrush the textured sections to achieve additional depth. This is done by using a brush with a minimal amount of paint on it. Lightly sweep the highest points with the brush.

11 Reposition the stencil and paint in desired areas. Additionally, use the wooden end of a paintbrush to draw lines in the paint.

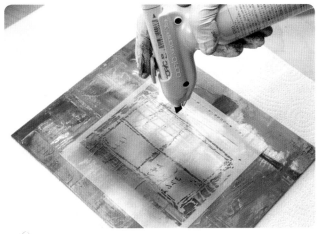

12 Switch to another stencil and use a Copic airbrush to spray ink in desired areas of the stencil. (Cover your work surface with paper towels if you're worried about overspray.)

13 Switch stencils again and add some glue with your finger in desired spots.

14 Dust some mica into the areas with glue. Press the mica into the glue to ensure it adheres. Remove the stencil and clean the mica off of it.

15 Dip an Inktense pencil into water and use it to add writing, drawing or outlining to your project. In this case, I added an outline around the mica. Inktense pencils can be activated with water to create a fluid, watercolor-like pigment that dries permanent.

16 Add some depth to the color by rubbing some fluid acrylics on the board with a damp paper towel.

17 Continue to reposition the stencils as desired and add additional layers of color. You can use your finger or a cosmetic sponge as an applicator.

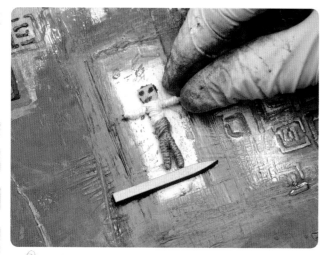

18 You may choose to add a three-dimensional object to your piece, using glue to adhere. Here, I chose a little man and a wood base for him to stand on.

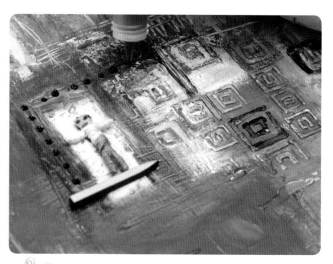

19 Add some final accents with Scribbles paint, which can be dispensed directly from its container. It has a nice, pointy tip so you can draw and write with it.

### *Fly Away Home*

Another Claybord painting, *Fly Away Home* also utilizes stencils as compositional elements, except with color instead of texture. The deep brick red is used sparingly with the Rafters stencil and succeeds in guiding the viewer's eye around the painting.

### *Promise Long*

Painted on wood panel instead of Claybord, this piece also shows how stencils can be used with texture to provide compositional elements to your piece. The Greek Key stencil, seen in the opposing corners, does just that.

### *Navigate* by Mary C. Nasser

Mary created this piece by starting with a stretched canvas that she primed with Matisse background colors. She then used a stencil from Artistcellar and sprayed over it with Liquitex spray paint. She collaged a vintage map and painted with acrylic paints, including DecoArt Fierro (in Gold), to add a glittering iron like texture. Finally, she added a metal ephemera arrow.

### *December Day* by Pam Carriker

Working on watercolor paper, Pam collaged a dictionary page with Mixed Media Adhesive and marked off her stencil area with water-soluble pencil, then whitewashed the area outside the stencil. She also added additional collage elements. She stenciled a design on deli paper with permanent Liquid Pencil. The face image (Pam Carriker Poetic Portrait Stamp Collection) was created with StazOn ink in a window of the stencil design. Other collage, including the deli paper, was added. The body was painted with watercolor paints and the background with PanPastels. The permanent Liquid Pencil was used to create dots, which can be burnished to a sheen. Final details were done with a white pen.

# Woulda Coulda Burn Wood

The rustic nature of wood-burned art always has a classic, yet somewhat naive appeal, and with stencils, you can achieve a lovely result right from the start. I'll be frank: The project shown here is an absolute first-time effort for me. And I loved it because the stencils did all the work. I do know that I will be making more of this type of work because I had a lot of fun doing it and the effect is quite nice.

Before you start this project, take a minute or two and gather stencils that can be put together to help you create a composition or scene. I chose two stencils, a tree and a bird, and that is all I used. Because the wood grain itself comes into play, I wanted to select stencils that would be enhanced by a wood-grain texture. Let's get started!

## WHAT YOU NEED

- *wood panel*
- *sandpaper*
- *stencil*
- *pencil*
- *wood-burning tool with shading tip*
- *razor blade or craft knife*
- *fluid acrylic paints*
- *paper towels*
- *Derwent Inktense black pencil*

## Here's a Tip

Wood-burning tools offer a variety of tips, and I tried them all out. The wood-burning tool itself operates easily. Press lightly, and you get a light line with a shallow burn mark. Press harder, and the wood burns deeper, and you get a darker line. After I got the hang of it, I found the shading tip was absolutely my favorite tool, probably because it mimics the feel of a brush. This tip can be manipulated in a side-to-side motion that results in a loose, gestural mark. In addition, you can still burn directly with the point of the tool. Consequently, I never found it necessary to even change tips; I used the shading tip for everything. Practice on scrap wood to find the tip that feels most comfortable for you.

1 Begin by sanding a birch panel (or any piece of wood that is not primed) in both directions so the wood is perfectly smooth. Don't skimp on this part, or your wood-burning tool might get caught in the grain later.

2 Trace a tree branch stencil onto the wood. Note: Do not burn the wood through the stencil, or the stencil will melt.

3 Using a wood-burning tool, burn the traced outline. Note: Even though stencils have breaks in them that disconnect the parts, you can ignore those in the pencil tracing and burn to create a cohesive image.

## Here's a Tip

If you make a mistake, run a sharp razor over that part. It works as an eraser!

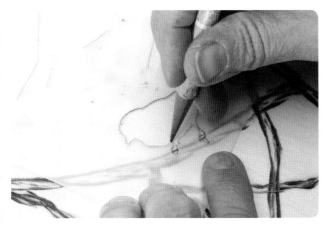

4 Trace a stencil of a bird sitting on one of the branches.

5 Remove the stencil and burn the lines of the bird. Choose your paint palette of fluid acrylics and water down the paint. Using a damp paper towel, begin brushing the paint over the wood like a stain. Apply the paint with the grain of the wood for subtle color.

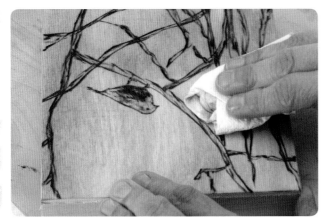

6 Don't worry about exact placement of the color. I used Golden Fluid Acrylics in Cobalt Turquoise, Quinacridone/ Nickel Azo Gold and Micaceous Iron Oxide.

7 Touch up your bird with an Inktense black pencil.

### *Autumn Song* by Margaret Applin

Margaret created *Autumn Song* by layering acrylic paints directly on birch plywood and then removing various levels of the paint through a hand-cut stencil. Screen-printed deli paper was attached to the pine wood pieces using decoupage medium, and the edges were touched up using Tim Holtz Distress Ink (Vintage Photo). Small holes were drilled in the corners of the painted plywood, and heavy-gauge, pounded-copper wire pieces were secured using light-gauge copper wire from the back side.

# Unmask That Paper Doll

Remember cutting paper dolls? In this project we are going to use them as a *painting mask*, which is a stencil in reverse. Using a mask is a cool way to create an interesting effect in your work. From scrapbook pages to journals to paintings, basically anything you can cut out can be used as a mask. And keep in mind that you can use both parts of whatever you are cutting. You can cut out the dolls, and then save the scrap and use it in another project.

Stencils and masks aren't just for paint, you know. We are going to incorporate some other media as well, layering compatibly with acrylics to create additional depth. And finally, we will learn to use limited parts of stencils and evaluate them for their design qualities, not necessarily their overall effect.

Stencils and masks work together like peanut butter and jelly or peanut butter and chocolate—depending on your preference. I love them any which way.

## WHAT YOU NEED

- *canvas panel, 12" x 12" (30cm x 30cm)*
- *gel medium*
- *glue brush*
- *collage elements*
- *white gesso*
- *stencils*
- *acrylic paints*
- *paintbrushes*
- *lightweight paper (copy paper)*
- *pencil*
- *scissors*
- *washi tape*
- *spray stencil adhesive*
- *PanPastels*
- *cosmetic sponge*
- *foam brushes*
- *acrylic sealer (such as Pam Carriker's Mixed Media Adhesive)*
- *Derwent Inktense pencil*
- *sequin waste (punchinella)*

1 Select random vintage collage text and glue to a canvas panel using gel medium. Apply glue underneath and on top of the collage papers.

2 Put a layer of white gesso over the whole canvas to make it more cohesive.

## Here's a Tip

When applying paper collage elements, lightly spritz both sides with water to prevent air bubbles. This will loosen the fibers so the paper "grabs" your substrate much better. Apply gel medium to the canvas first, then your paper, then additional gel medium on top.

3 Place a stencil on top of the substrate and randomly apply paint, varying the amount.

4 Fold a piece of lightweight paper accordion style and make hand-cut paper dolls by drawing an outline of half a person on the folded edge.

5 Cut around the outline.

6 When considering what to add next, you might lay out elements on your canvas without adhering them. Play with them like puzzle pieces to see what arrangement looks best.

7 Adhere elements such as washi tape or additional collage elements, but don't adhere the paper dolls just yet. Adding little stenciled sections after each collage element helps integrate things and create additional depth.

24    Sign up for our free newsletter at www.CreateMixedMedia.com.

8 Spray stencil adhesive on the paper dolls and then position them on the painting. Apply acrylic paint over the paper dolls, using them as a reverse stencil.

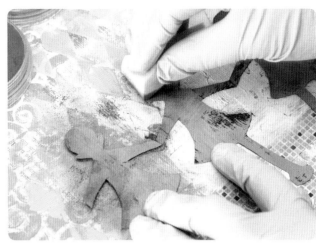

9 Using a cosmetic sponge, dab pastels around the paper dolls. Smudge the pastels in other areas of the painting to create a cohesive effect.

10 Dab a layer of acrylic sealer over the top of the pastel areas to seal it and prevent it from smudging.

11 Gently lift the paper doll mask from the piece. If you have trouble getting the first edge, use the tip of your scissors to lift the first bit. Save the painted paper dolls for use in another project.

12 Add another stencil on top of your painting. Paint over the stencil using fluid acrylics and a foam brush. Note that only a portion of this stencil is used, just to create an archway.

13 Remove the stencil. Flip it upside down and add the stencil in a different part of your painting.

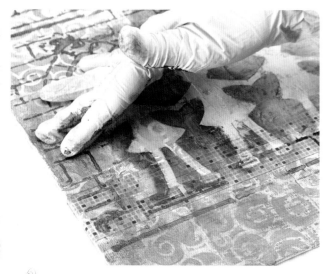

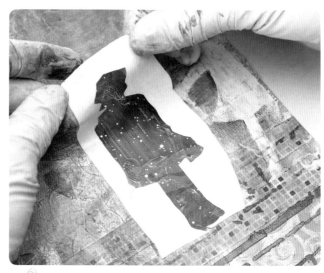

**14** Remove the stencil. Add layers of paint as desired using your fingers or a brush.

**15** Add some collage elements to your piece, including the silhouette of a person. Position the image so it replaces one of the negative spaces left by the dolls. I used an image of myself as a child for this.

**16** Add more painting around the piece as you see fit, including details to the paper doll girls to enhance their differences, such as painting them different colors or framing areas around them. Using an Inktense pencil, outline the girls.

**17** Finally, add some stenciling around the borders if you like using punchinella.

### *Silence* by Seth Apter

Seth worked on watercolor paper to create his background using layers of white gesso and multiple colors of acrylic paint and acrylic glazes. He used a variety of stencils, spray paint and mist ink. The main tree image (from a stencil by Ed Roth—www.stencil1.com) was created using a palette knife to spread fiber paste through the stencil. He created drips at the top with a loaded stencil brush, pouncing several colors of heavy body acrylics through a stencil. Multiple colors of acrylic paint and glazes were layered on a sheet of Tyvek, and he used an alphabet stencil to make his letters.

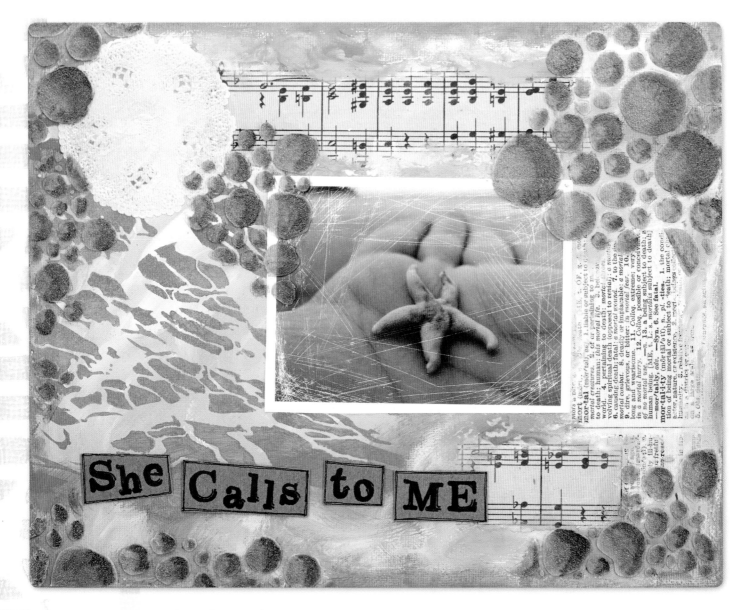

### *She Calls to Me* by Lisa Cousineau

Lisa used a "surf" stencil in the traditional way in the background with paint. On top of her picture, she pushed coarse molding paste through a "sea foam" stencil and let it dry. The piece was finished with iridescent paints over the molding paste. The stencils in this piece are by Artistcellar.

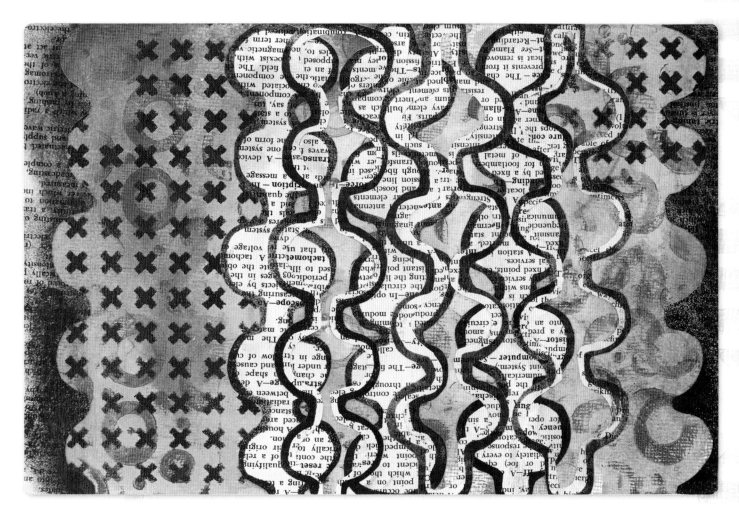

## Bonus Project

I was in a funky mid-century modern mood when I made this piece. I started by drawing freehand shapes on contact paper. I used the shapes as both stencils and masks, using acrylic paint and creating the collage elements with the stencils, too.

You can see step-by-step instructions for this project at www.CreateMixedMedia.com/stencilgirl.

Sign up for our free newsletter at **www.CreateMixedMedia.com.**

# Magazine Magic

The vast majority of my art is labor-intensive. Paintings that I work over and over, alternatively struggling, rejoicing, repeating often for days and even months before all the layers are finished. I have often joked that a project isn't done until I have bled on it, as if I had to suffer for it to be right. This is not one of those projects.

This project uses stencils as rubbing plates underneath magazine pages. And it is indeed magical how quickly you can create a seemingly complex background. I selected my pages from decorating magazines and have found that some pages make better rubbings than others. Play around until you find out what works best for you.

These backgrounds are so fun and easy you'll find yourself tearing pages out of magazines and saving them for later use. In one work session, you can make a  bunch of rubbings at a time to build a supply of collage elements.

## WHAT YOU NEED

- *magazines*
- *stencils*
- *sandpaper*
- *acrylic paint*
- *palette knife*
- *canvas board, matboard or any flat substrate*
- *gel medium or collage medium (such as Pam Carriker's Mixed Media Adhesive)*
- *paintbrush*
- *craft knife*
- *Thermofax screen (optional)*
- *screen-printing squeegee*

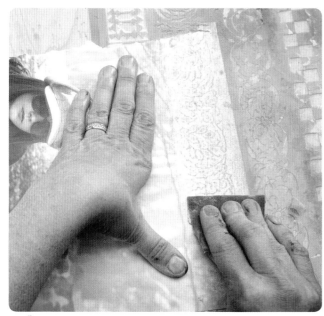

1 Select some pages from a magazine. Lay a page on top of a stencil and sand the magazine paper lightly, using sandpaper. The outline of the stencil image will show through. Experiment with fine-grit and rougher sandpapers to see which effect you like best. Sand enough pages to create a series of horizontal strips that will go across the board.

2 Mix up a background color that will coordinate with your magazine pages and paint the board. This is just in case your torn strips don't line up sufficiently.

3 Using gel medium or collage medium, adhere your sanded strips to the board.

4 Allow the collage to dry, then turn the board over and trim the excess paper from the edges with a craft knife.

5 Set your Thermofax screen over your collaged board. I chose a screen designed by Margaret Applin, but you can easily substitute a stencil. If you are using a screen, spread a thick line of fluid acrylic at the top of the screen. (I used Micaceous Iron Oxide) on the top edge as shown.

6 Pull the paint down over the screen using a screen-printing squeegee or other spreader.

7 Remove the Thermofax screen.

## Here's a Tip

A Thermofax is like a small silkscreen except it's not silk; it is polyester. I consider them cousins to stencils. They are similar in that they allow the artist to create a repeated image over and over. They differ, though, because the Thermofax screen, by its nature, allows more detail than a stencil, so fine lines are better replicated. There are several places where you can buy ready-made screens and also where you can have your own images put onto screens. I have listed those in the Resources (www.CreateMixedMedia.com/stencilgirl). Use them alone or in combination with stencils.

## Removing Gridlock

Using sandpaper is what I call a removal process, in that you create by taking away. For this project, I used a Mr. Clean Magic Eraser, which is another type of removal process.

You can see step-by-step instructions for this project at www.CreateMixedMedia.com/stencilgirl.

Sign up for our free newsletter at **www.CreateMixedMedia.com.**

# How Can You Resist a Fish?

**W**e already know it is very effective to use stencils to add paint and other media to your projects, but what if you used stencils to actually remove paint? In this project we create a collaged painting that utilizes several different techniques that all result in slightly different effects.

Resists often build on the idea of removal such as that which was presented in the last project. But instead of removing paint or magazine imagery, this time we use a variety of mediums with stencils to actually prevent or *resist* the application of paint.

There are lots of different products that will work, ranging from gel medium to hand sanitizer to wax. We are using bleach and gesso, but don't be afraid to play a bit more with these techniques. Play with layering up resist over resist like we do here. I think you will find they are pretty irresistible.

## WHAT YOU NEED

- *stencils*
- *black text-weight paper*
- *Clorox Bleach Pen*
- *paper plate*
- *foam brush*
- *scissors*
- *white gesso*
- *canvas board*
- *Silks Acrylic Glaze*
- *paintbrushes*
- *paper towels*
- *baby wipes*
- *watercolor paint*
- *collage medium (such as Pam Carriker's Mixed Media Adhesive)*
- *bottle cap*

1 Place a fish stencil on a piece of black text-weight paper. Dispense part of a Clorox Bleach Pen on a paper plate. Using a foam brush, dab the bleach onto the stencil. It may take the bleach a bit to start taking effect on the paper.

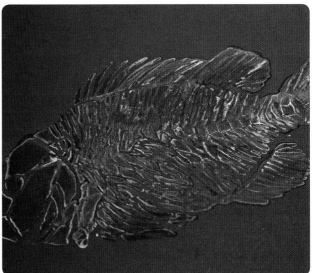

2 Rinse the stencil. Your fish is now ready to cut out.

**3** Using a foam brush, apply white gesso over a stencil onto a canvas substrate. Once the gesso is dry, apply a layer of Silks Acrylic Glaze over the entire piece.

**4** Wipe off the excess paint with a paper towel. Use a baby wipe to rub the paint off of the gessoed areas.

**5** Apply a layer of gesso on a piece of paper through a stencil. Allow the gesso to dry.

**6** Paint over the stenciled page with watercolor.

**7** Cut out the fish and some of the blue tree parts. Collage them on the canvas substrate using collage medium (such as Pam Carriker's Mixed Media Adhesive).

**8** Stencil a school of some baby fish onto the collage.

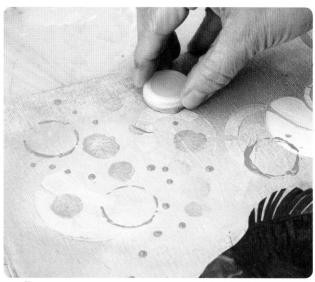

 Think outside the box and use stencils in a way they aren't intended. For instance, use flower stems as seaweed!

 Stamp with a bottle cap to create large bubbles

11 Add smaller bubbles with the end of a paintbrush. Fill in any final bubbles for the fish using a circle stencil.

## Here's a Tip

Wiping paint off of gesso is largely a matter of personal preference. You can dab here and there for a mottled effect or completely remove the paint to reveal pops of white. Play with both methods and mix it up. Glossy gel medium can be used in a similar way to the gesso. Since gel medium is clear, the underneath color will be exposed, so plan accordingly.

Sign up for our free newsletter at **www.CreateMixedMedia.com.**

# Let's Get Dimensional

**A**s a mixed-media painter, I typically work on a two-dimensional substrate—painting and building up layers but rarely actually jumping off the substrate. And I certainly never get sculptural in the true sense of the word. I do manage to amuse myself, though, by making three-dimensional parts out of clay, wood or other found objects.

We have already seen how stencils can be used to create texture in mixed-media pieces. Let's take a look at how you can use stencils to make objects that are quasi-pop-up in appearance, which can then be incorporated into your work. In this project we are going to use stencils in conjunction with clay and built-up paper to find extra dimension. The addition of such parts can ramp up your work in a variety of ways. You could even choose to make true dioramas or shadow boxes with these techniques.

## WHAT YOU NEED

- *bristol or watercolor paper*
- *Wood Icing*
- *canvas panel*
- *palette knife*
- *air-dry clay*
- *clay roller*
- *craft knife*
- *stencils*
- *pencil*
- *acrylic paint*
- *paintbrushes*
- *stencil brush*
- *foam plate or foam sheet*
- *stylus*
- *brayer*
- *black marker*
- *white gesso*
- *fabric scrap*
- *craft glue*
- *toothpicks or pop dots*

1. Start with a piece of bristol paper (don't use cardstock) or watercolor paper. Spread a layer of Wood Icing over the paper in a consistently thin layer. You don't want a rough surface, so try to keep it smooth. Allow this to dry and then repeat on the other side. You will have a hefty yet pliable non-cracking substrate.

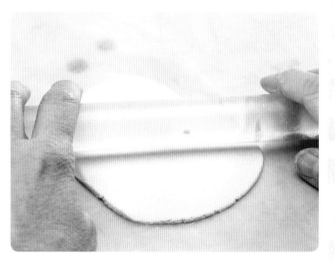

2. While your Wood Icing paper is drying, roll air-dry clay into a flat piece about ¼" (6mm) or so thick.

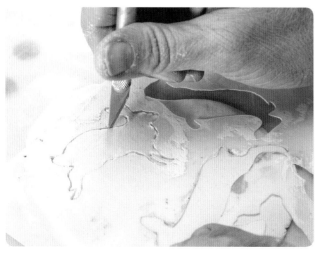

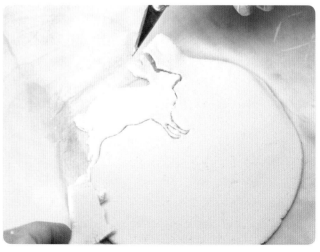

3 Lay down your animal stencil. Using a craft knife, cut out the animal. A gentle up-and-down, rather than dragging, motion works best.

4 Tear away the excess clay and reshape as necessary. Repeat for as many animals as you'd like in your diorama.

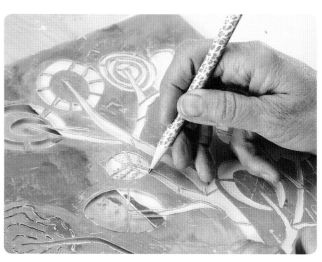

5 Add a little bit of extra clay to the body of the animal to give it some more depth and realism. Allow the animal to dry thoroughly.

6 Choose a stencil for your whimsical trees and trace them onto the Wood-Iced paper using a pencil.

7 Paint the stenciled trees using acrylic paint and a fine paint-brush. Allow the trees to dry.

8 Cut out the painted Wood-Iced components.

9 Now that you have some component parts ready, it is time to start working on the canvas panel. Using an all-over pattern stencil, paint some hills.

10 Use a stencil to simulate rays of sunshine or a sunset from behind your hillside.

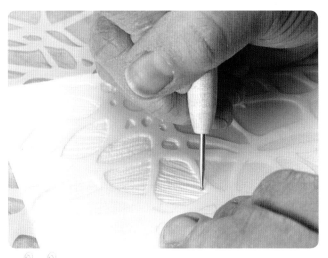

11 Cut a piece of foam material (such as a foam plate) to a small, manageable size. Place the stencil used for the hills on the foam. Use a stylus to press down the foam in the spaces of the stencil—almost like carving them away. This creates a negative image of the stencil.

12 Ink up the foam plate you created by rolling a brayer of paint on it.

## Here's a Tip

Using a foam plate to create a negative of your stencils is a terrific way to inexpensively expand their usage. It's like two stencils for one! You could even create the negative in a specific shape if you so desire. Imagine cutting a cloud shape and then turning that into a textured stamp. You will be able to paint much more interesting layers this way.

13 Press the painted foam plate on your board and use it as a stamp to add texture to the hills.

**14** Before attaching the Wood-Iced components, touch up the edges with a black marker.

**15** Paint the rabbit cutout bright white with gesso.

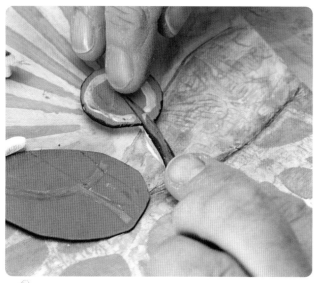

**16** Arrange your components in the desired composition on the board. Give your bunny a scarf using a scrap of fabric. Fringe the edges by cutting little slits at the scarf ends. Start gluing the components down using any kind of heavy craft glue.

**17** Add more depth to some of the objects by using toothpicks or pop dots behind them. Add any final details with paint and a fine brush.

### *Wood Triptych* by Laurie Mika

Laurie started out with a plain wood triptych and applied Wood Icing on top of stencils over the door panels on both sides. She then painted a base coat of a black/brown over the entire triptych and wiped back the raised sections that had the Wood Icing. She used another stencil on the center panel and lightly dabbed paint on it to be very subtle in the background. She applied silver gilder's paste over the Wood Icing to highlight those areas and to simulate a metal appearance. Laurie made all the pieces in this triptych from polymer clay or resin and molds, and glued them in place. She also used a stencil on the raw clay (toward the bottom).

She rolled out a slab of silver polymer clay and pushed the stencil into the clay and rolled over it with a rolling pin so it produced a raised image. She painted the image with acrylic paint and then used the gilder's paste once again to highlight the raised surface design. Finally, she baked it in the oven.

### Air-Dry Pendant Bonus Project

When Laurie's project arrived, I squealed with delight because it is absolutely gorgeous (for one thing) and such a departure from the type of work I typically make (for another thing). I decided to try my hand at a clay pendant (using air-dry Critter Clay) by pushing a stencil into the clay as Laurie did.

You can see step-by-step instruction for this project at www.CreateMixedMedia.com/stencilgirl.

# Wax and Waning Encaustic

A couple of years ago, I added encaustic painting to my bag of tricks. Oh my, how I love the smell of beeswax. It seems that stencils and wax are perfect partners—especially when the stencils are made of Mylar, which is heat tolerant. In fact, when using stencils, layers of encaustic wax work just as beautifully as any paint or other mixed-media product.

I have chosen to use a few stencils that coordinate with one another—positive and negative designs in different sizes. This will allow me to exploit the layering power of pattern on pattern. One of the keys to using pattern successfully is to stick with a pattern but vary the size. For instance, if you are using damask shapes, stick with all damask; don't throw in a fleur-de-lis.

Although I started with a primed Encausticbord, you could make this project on unprimed wood because the tar will offer plenty of adhesion for the subsequent wax layers. When working with encaustics, be sure to fuse between each layer, and always work in a room with adequate ventilation and plenty of fresh airflow.

## WHAT YOU NEED

- *Mylar stencils (heat-tolerant), 2 or 3 coordinating patterns*
- *wood substrate*
- *palette knife*
- *tar or asphalt patching compound (water-soluble)*
- *baby wipes*
- *encaustic palette/heat source*
- *encaustic paint*
- *clear encaustic medium*
- *paraffin wax (for cleaning brushes)*
- *natural bristle brushes*
- *blowtorch or heat gun*
- *soft lint-free rag or Viva paper towels*
- *craft knife or sharp tool for carving wax*
- *oil stick*
- *blending stick (or Crisco oil)*
- *gloves*
- *amber shellac (optional)*

1 Place a stencil on your board. Using a palette knife, spread a layer of tar over the whole piece. Remove the stencil and clean it immediately using a baby wipe or damp paper towel. Allow the tar to dry thoroughly; this could take thirty minutes or so. This is a good time to preheat your encaustic palette.

2 Your encaustic palette and medium should be heated up by now to approximately 175°F, no higher than 200°F (79°C–93°C). Place your dry tarred piece on the palette to warm it up, which will make it more receptive to the hot wax.

3 Paint a layer of encaustic medium onto your piece.

4 Fuse the wax with a blowtorch. Add two more layers of medium, fusing in between.

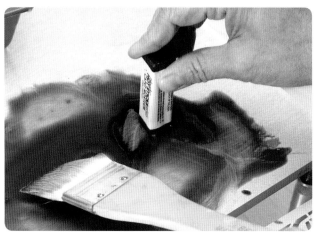

5 Melt some encaustic paint (color of your choice) onto your heated palette.

6 Place a stencil on your piece and paint a layer over the piece. You can mix different colors on your heated palette, and you can add a bit of the clear medium to the color to reduce the opacity.

## Here's a Tip

Wipe your palette clean using a paper towel. You can also place your stencil on the griddle to melt the wax to wipe it clean. (The stencil will not melt if you're using a StencilGirl stencil!)

7 Carefully peel off the stencil to reveal your design.

8 Lightly and quickly fuse your stenciled design with a blow-torch. Don't heat it too much, which will melt the wax completely, because you want to retain the pattern.

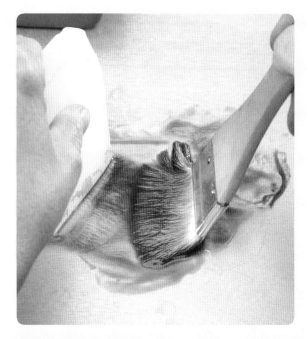

9 Paint another layer of clear encaustic medium on your project.

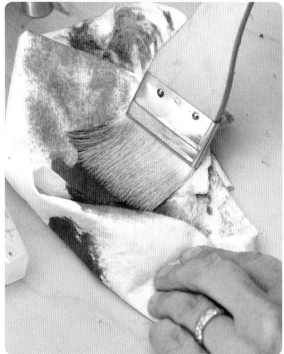

## Here's a Tip

Clean your brush in melted paraffin wax and wipe it on a paper towel to get the colored medium out of it.

10 Torch the wax to fuse it again.

11 Air bubbles will appear and burst as you torch. You may choose to fill in those holes with drops of wax using a fine-pointed brush. If you do, torch again.

12 Add an opposing stencil to your project. Choose another color of wax. Paint a layer of the color on the stencil.

13 Carefully remove the stencil and fuse. Always fuse between every coat of paint.

14 Switch stencils and add another layer to your painting. Carefully remove the stencil and fuse again using a torch.

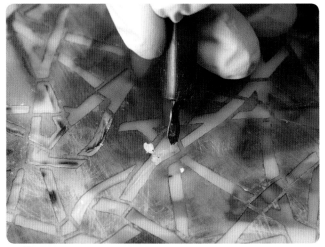

15 Paint another layer of clear encaustic medium on the whole project and fuse. Add a stencil on top of your painting and use a sharp object to carve inside the stencil. You may choose to use different stencils on different areas of your painting for carving.

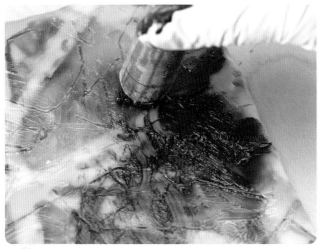

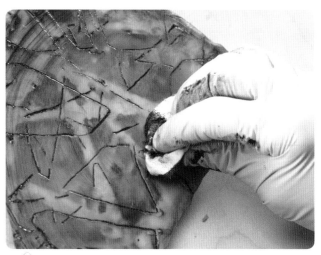

**16** Rub an oil stick or a small amount of oil paint over the painting, making sure it gets down into the carved areas. Use a blending stick (or Crisco oil) first and the oil stick will spread more easily. Make sure you wear gloves for this process.

**17** Wipe the excess paint off the piece with a clean paper towel.

**18** Fuse your wax with the torch. To clean up the edges of your painting, set them on the palette to melt the wax off.

**19** OPTIONAL: Add an amber shellac torching. Use your palette knife to add a layer of shellac to your piece.

**20** Light fire to the shellac and let it burn until the flame goes out. It's best to do this part outdoors for ventilation purposes.

### Eddy Meets the Rose

This encaustic was made using a similar process. I omitted the tar and I only used one stencil. It kind of amazes me how interesting a piece can become when the pattern is limited. In this case, I just kept moving the stencil around to capture different parts and create additional layers. The shellac-burn formed shapes that echo the stencil.

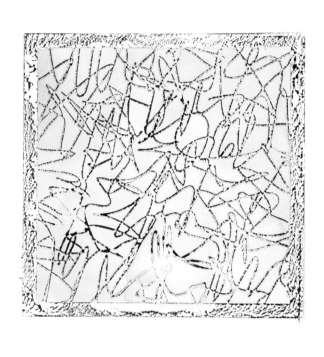

### *Untitled* by Wendy Aikin

Wendy's piece is an example of an encaustic stencil transfer. Wendy started by melting silver encaustic paint onto a warm palette. The stencil was laid in the wax, lifted up and placed on a silicone mat (also sitting on the warm palette). Rives BFK paper was laid on top of the stencil, and the encaustic was transferred from the stencil to the paper. When the paper was lifted, the encaustic remained on the paper, creating a resist. The area was then given a wash of yellow watercolor.

### *Infinite Unity* by Julie Snidle

Julie made this encaustic piece in several layers. After priming the 8" x 8" (30cm x 30cm) wood panel with three coats of beeswax, encaustic paint was applied using a stencil to create the designs. Clear encaustic medium was used between the layers of pigmented wax to achieve additional depth. Black India ink was used on the top layer as a flourish.

### *Iterations #6* by Lisa Sisley-Blinn

Lisa created an encaustic painting on a cradled panel. She used hand-cut stencils as a guide for incised lines, which were filled with oil stick. She also used the hand-cut stencils for low-relief encaustic areas and some gold leaf shapes.

### *Pattern Play* by Julie Snidle
### Bonus Project

Another way to use a stencil on an encaustic piece is illustrated on this painting. The background was created before the stencil was applied. Julie taped off the approximate width of the border stencil that she intended to use. This allowed a nice, crisp line. First, she painted over the stencil with one color of encaustic paint. She allowed this to cool, set the stencil aside and then painted over the textured stencil part with another color. Once that had cooled, she carefully scraped away the top layer of wax to reveal the stenciled design, now shown in two colors. She removed the tape and did a quick fuse.

You can see a stepped-out version of this project at www.CreateMixedMedia.com/stencilgirl.

# STENCIL DÉCOR

*I have never been one of those people who makes her own household items. Except for scrubbies and dishcloths (which I knit) and my artwork on the walls, I rarely make things for my house. I have been hesitant because of my own perceived lack of ability. But the more I use stencils in my work, the more I realize they are the perfect tools to use to customize décor items.*

Think about all the home décor pieces you see online and in design stores. So many of them can easily be replicated with the use of stencils. Pillow covers, place mats, lamp shades and more! What is even better is that you can not only replicate, but also improve these projects by picking colors that complement your own home.

Who but artists could even conceive of all the options?

# Can-Can Lantern

In this project we will use a stencil as a template for hole punching. We are using a metal can from a hardware store, which is also where I got the idea to make a can into a lantern. You could also apply this same hole-punching technique to a lot of other substrates such as plastic or leather, and I am sure you will think of tons of ideas that are not candle related. I used a real candle inside this Can-Can Lantern, but you could use a battery-powered candle if you are worried about a fire risk.

I am sure you will think of tons of variations such as spray painting the can first or using fabric trim. I want to use the Can-Can Lantern outdoors so I deliberately kept it simple. The contrast of the metal can with just a little bit of glitz pleases my sense of juxtaposition. I think that several of these lanterns would look really cool hanging on shepherd's hooks around the patio.

## WHAT YOU NEED

- *metal can*
- *stencils*
- *duct tape or gaffer's tape*
- *large or medium nail*
- *hammer*
- *awl*
- *sequins*
- *glue*

**1** Fill your metal can with water and freeze. This will help retain the shape of the can while you punch.

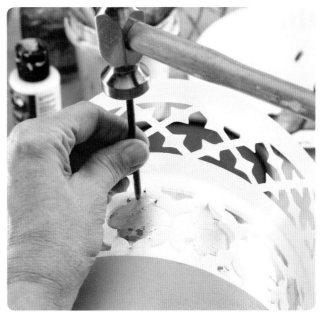

**2** Adhere your stencil using strong tape, such as duct tape or gaffer's tape. Use a large nail and hammer to punch holes around the anchor points of the stencil.

**3** Use a smaller nail or awl for the detailed areas to create a unique effect that will really pop when light shines through.

**4** Finish punching your design and let the ice melt out before decorating. Decide how you're going to decorate your lantern. I added some different sized and colored sequins to add to the Moroccan theme. If you're going to use your lantern outdoors, be sure to use appropriate glue.

## Here's a Tip

Start punching holes at the top. As the ice melts, it might start to leak through the lower holes. Refreeze as often as needed.

## Yupo Candle Sleeves
## Bonus Project

If you can't get enough of candles (and I know I can't), you can easily make sleeves out of Yupo paper. Stencil directly onto the paper with acrylic paint and then trim to size. Easy and cute.

You can see step-by-step instruction for this project at www.CreateMixedMedia.com/stencilgirl.

### Etched Stencil Cuff Bracelets by Jen Cushman

Jen did her etching with a chemical process of dipping base metals in ferric chloride. She placed the stencil on brass and then used StazOn ink over the top to create the pattern. After letting the ink dry, she dipped the metal into the ferric chloride for thirty minutes. Then she cleaned off the etchant solution and added a patina.

### *Winter Bird* by Leighanna Light

Leighanna calls this technique *faux etching* which can be done using copper, brass or steel. Apply matte medium over your stencil onto the metal. When it is dry, brush Novacan Black Patina over the entire piece and allow to dry.

## Copper Button Keeper Bonus Project

The minute I saw Leighanna's project, I knew I had to try this
faux etching. I quickly ordered the Novacan online and repeated
Leighanna's instructions to create this little Button Keeper plaque.

You can see step-by-step instruction for this project at
www.CreateMixedMedia.com/stencilgirl.

# Felt-A-Rama

**Y**ou can do so many things with felt. I am forever scavenging at thrift stores to snatch up the good wool sweaters. I think Shetland wool tends to felt better than something like merino or cashmere. I also buy men's sweaters because you get more fabric out of them. To make the wool felt, all you need to do is wash the sweaters in your machine on a hot, soapy cycle, then dry on hot. It works better if you wash several sweaters at the same time. The felting actually occurs as they get tossed around in the washer, so the more, the merrier. If the sweater doesn't felt up enough when you first try it, just wash it again. You are going for a fabric (of sorts) that will not unravel when you cut into it.

Keep in mind that you can cut the felt into any shape. You could use stencils as a guide for cutting and then felting. Squares of mix-and-match stenciled and felted material make terrific scarves, purses, coasters, place mats, tree skirts, blankets, table runners, or whatever!

## WHAT YOU NEED

- *100% wool sweater*
- *rotary cutter*
- *cutting mat*
- *ruler*
- *stencil*
- *straight pins*
- *wool roving*
- *felting needles*
- *wool yarn*
- *scissors*

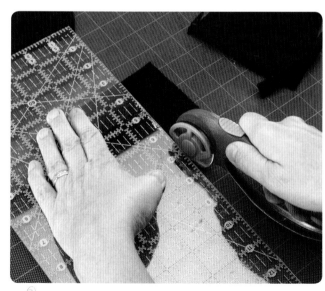

**1** Buy a wool sweater at Goodwill or your favorite thrift store. Wash it in super-hot water and machine dry to shrink it. Cut a 4" x 4" (10cm x 10cm) square of the sweater using a rotary cutter.

**2** Place your stencil on the square of fabric and hold it in place using pins.

**3** Using the stencil as your guide, add colored roving. I kind of eyeballed what I was doing and then moved the stencil. Use a felting needle to poke up and down until the roving becomes one with the felt (you will be able to see this if you turn the piece over). Start slow; there's no need to rush. This will hopefully prevent you from poking your finger with the needle (ask me how I know).

**4** After you're finished with the main shapes, add wool yarn for linear parts. Attach it with the felting needle the same way you did with the roving.

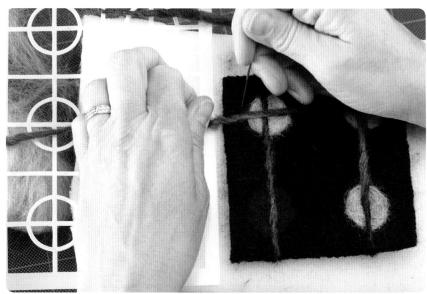

## Here's a Tip

Have a hole in your nice wool sweater? Use a felting tool to fix it! First, mend the hole with a similar color roving. Then create an interesting design over the top of this area and elsewhere on your sweater. You will end up with a totally altered new look. I have even intentionally bought a sweater with holes just for this purpose.

**5** Trim the excess yarn from the edges when you are finished. And make plans for your next project.

### Clutch Purse by Joanne Sharpe

This clutch purse could easily be replicated with felted material instead of the layers of hand-painting that Joanne did, using a stencil as her guide. She then did free-form quilting over the top, using the same stencil as a guide. There are felting attachments for some sewing machines that would allow you to do something similar with wool. True story: Joanne had intended this to be a wall hanging until she was folding it up to mail to me. She called and said, oh my gosh, it would be a super-cute clutch purse. Naturally I agreed, and when it arrived at my house, I pretty much begged her to give it to me because it is so darn cute. I am shameless.

# Spray It Again, Sam

During the years that I did outdoor art fairs, I was looking for a low-end product to sell. These shows usually required that all art be original, and I wanted something that I could make quickly enough for it to be profitable but that, of course, still looked good. One day I was walking around IKEA, saw some simple framed mirrors and that was all she wrote. I have made hundreds of these through the years. Back in the day, I used to cover our side yard with a tarp and drag my box of paints and stencils outside. I would set up this crazy-looking assembly line and get to work.

Once again, it is the layering process that really makes these pop. I pick a color scheme before I start and stick with it, usually two to three colors plus black or white. You can try whatever you like and see what works for you. As you can see, I substituted all sorts of items for commercial stencils this time around. I am sure you will be able to find lots of inexpensive "stencils" around your house, too. Onion bag, anyone?

## WHAT YOU NEED

- *mirror in a wood frame*
- *assorted stencils*
- *assorted spray paints*
- *scrap paper*
- *razor blade*

## Here's a Tip

As far as a paint-color strategy, remember your color wheel when picking paints. Analogous is always good, meaning colors that are next to each other. Split complementary is quite effective, too; instead of red and green (complementary), you would pick red and the color on each side of green. So in this example, you would pick red, blue-green and yellow-green. I love to "pop" the piece at the end with either black or white.

## Here's a Tip

I have found that it is quicker to just spray right over the mirror and scrape the paint off later than it is to tape it off.

1 Apply your first stencil, including improvisational stencils like fabric or doilies. Spray using your first color, move the stencil and keep going.

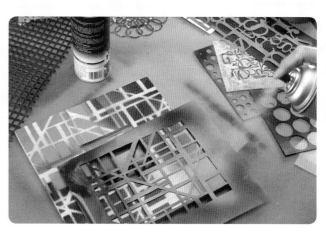

2 Move your stencil and spray using a different color.

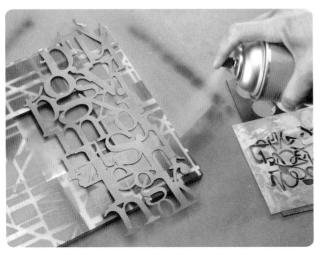

3 Choose a different stencil (in this case a partial piece of scrapbook paper). Spray using a new color or an already-used color.

4 Try using a piece of open canvas as your stencil. Spray in a new color.

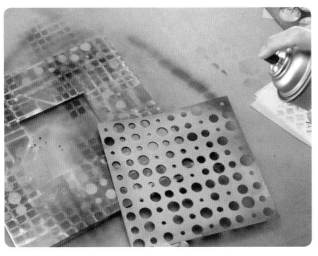

5 You can spray only portion of a stencil; you don't need to use all of it.

6 If you only want part of a stencil, cover all but that part with a piece of scrap paper. You can also layer stencils by putting one stencil with a smaller pattern under a stencil with a larger design.

7 After you've added all of your layers, finish off the top layer with a large flourish.

8 To finish, use a razor blade to scrape off the paint that has covered the mirror. You can also touch up the edges with black paint if you want.

### *Love Pattern* by Michelle Ward

Michelle prepped bristol board by covering it with several colors of acrylic spray paint (Liquitex and Montana). She use patterned stencils in multiple sizes and sprayed and monoprinted over the background. To emphasize the designs, some of the images were defined with a wipe-out method using acrylic paints. She added journaling with a white china grease pen, pencil and black paint pen.

### *Polka Dot Platter* by Carole Perry

Carole started with two 14" (36cm) circles of cut glass—one clear and one white. She stacked the plates and then sifted finely crushed glass over a stencil, changing the position of the stencil and also using three colors of powdered glass. The piece was fused in a kiln, cooled and then reheated and formed over a mold into the shape of a serving platter.

### Easy Etch Bonus Project

Using Armour Etch, I hand-cut a stencil from contact paper and etched a design into this recycled glass jar.

You can see step-by-step instructions for this project at www.CreateMixedMedia.com/stencilgirl.

Sign up for our free newsletter at www.CreateMixedMedia.com.

# Quilt Me Batik

I am smitten with batik. I pretty much love everything about it, from the beeswax to the beautiful patterns to the vintage wooden and copper tools that are often used. I imagine skilled artisans carefully making dye and crafting their intricate patterns to create luscious fabrics. The problem is that I don't really work with fabric very often, and I'm also a total novice at anything involving a sewing machine.

Imagine my delight when I learned that paper works beautifully with batik! My friend Katherine Engen, the owner of Valley Ridge Art Studio, taught me what she knew and told me to "run with it." And run I did, creating all sorts of new ways to make a batik effect on paper, including the methods I share here.

Although I typically use a tjanting to dispense wax, I have found that regular brushes offer a little bit more control when working with stencils. In this project, we will use stencils three ways. We will first create lovely batik papers, and then we will use a stencil to create a template for a paper quilt. Finally, we will use a stencil as our sewing guide.

## Here's a Tip

Many of my stencils are stained and look kind of yucky. That will generally not affect the outcome as the paint is long dried. You do, however, want to make sure the stencils are clean of dried wax. This is done by putting the stencil on a warm palette and wiping it clean.

## WHAT YOU NEED

- tape
- freezer paper
- stencils
- spray stencil adhesive (optional)
- unryu paper
- batik wax (beeswax or soy wax)
- brushes with natural bristles for use with wax
- watercolor paint, several colors
- watercolor paintbrushes
- drying rack
- newsprint
- iron/ironing board
- paper
- lightbox
- collage medium (such as Pam Carriker's Mixed Media Adhesive)
- needle and thread (optional)

1 Tape a piece of freezer paper to your table to prevent your paper from sticking to the surface. If desired, spray stencil adhesive to the back of your stencil to ensure that wax does not seep under the stencil. Press the stencil onto the unryu paper and paint a layer of batik wax over the stencil.

2 Carefully peel away the stencil. Repeat this on several pieces of paper using a variety of stencil designs. (You can also flick wax onto your papers to allow for random spots.)

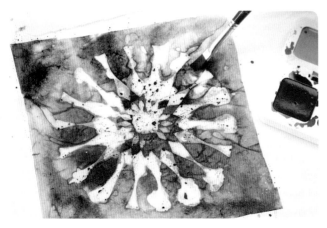

3 Using watercolor paints, start adding colors to the wax-stenciled paper. You may choose to use one large swath of color, but I prefer to use a variety of colors and let them bleed into one another. Continue to make batik papers until you feel like you have enough diversity to make a quilt. Place your papers on a drying rack to dry.

4 After the watercolor is dry, paint a layer of wax over the top of the entire paper. Allow this to cool. If desired, you can crumple the waxed paper and then drizzle ink or more watercolor (in a darker color) over the paper so it goes into the cracks.

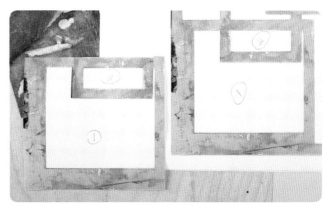

5 Sandwich the paper between two pieces of newsprint. Iron (at medium or high heat) until you see no more wax absorbed into the newsprint.

6 Use a contemporary stencil as the basis for your quilt. Make three photocopies of your stencil. As you cut your squares apart on one copy, number that square and the corresponding square on another copy so you know how to put your quilt back together.

7 Use the cutouts to choose which pieces of batiked papers you want to go where in your quilt. Cut out the shapes and lay them on the marked stencil. This is your preview and gives you a chance to see if the layout works. You may choose to leave some of the paper edges torn versus cut.

8 Place the substrate paper over the third photocopy and position on top of a lightbox so you can see the numbering guide. Using a brush, paint a layer of collage medium on the substrate and also on the back of the paper quilt piece. When you press the quilt piece into place, the papers will easily sandwich together. If desired, use another stencil to add a stitching guide and hand-sew in a contrasting color.

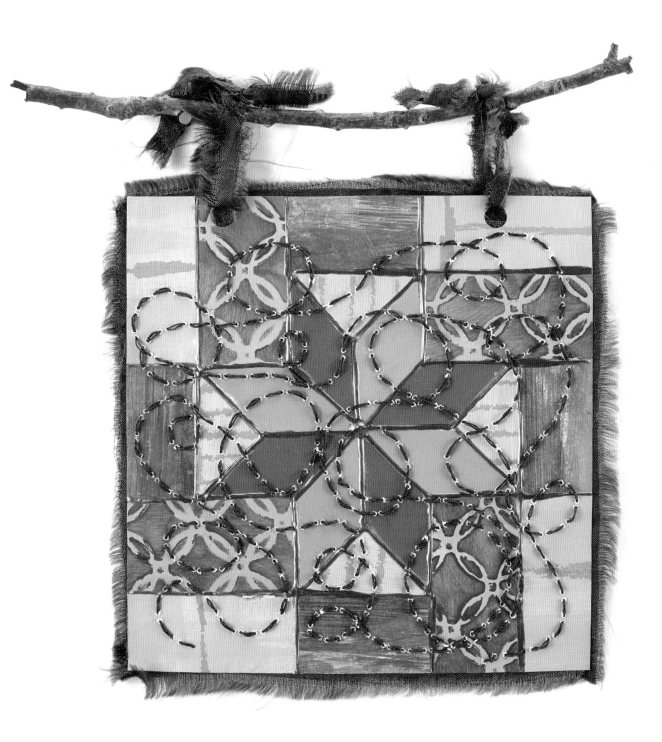

### Branching Out

This is another paper quilt that was painted on regular copy paper instead of unryu. I simply painted papers with acrylic paint rather than making batik paper. Stencils guided the paper painting and I stuck with a set color scheme but tried to create enough variation of my papers so they would be interesting. I wanted to simulate a folk-art look. After assembling, I used a stencil as a guide to add topstitching and I finished the piece by hanging it from a tree branch.

### *California Autumn* by Jane LaFazio

Jane began this piece by stenciling with acrylic ink on white and coffee-stained cloth. (These stencils are her own designs.) She then sewed the sections of cloth together and layered stenciled organza on top. Using the stencils as inspiration, she did machine free-motion stitching and finished up with hand-stitching.

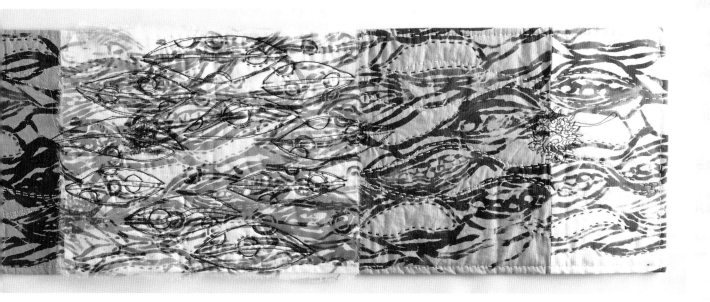

### *Doodle Mania* Bonus Project

You can create doodle templates simply by tracing a stencil onto a substrate and then creating doodles in each space. Another idea is to paint the background first using a stencil and then doodle in selected areas. Small stencils can even be used as the doodle, too!

You can see step-by-step instructions for this project at www.CreateMixedMedia. com/stencilgirl.

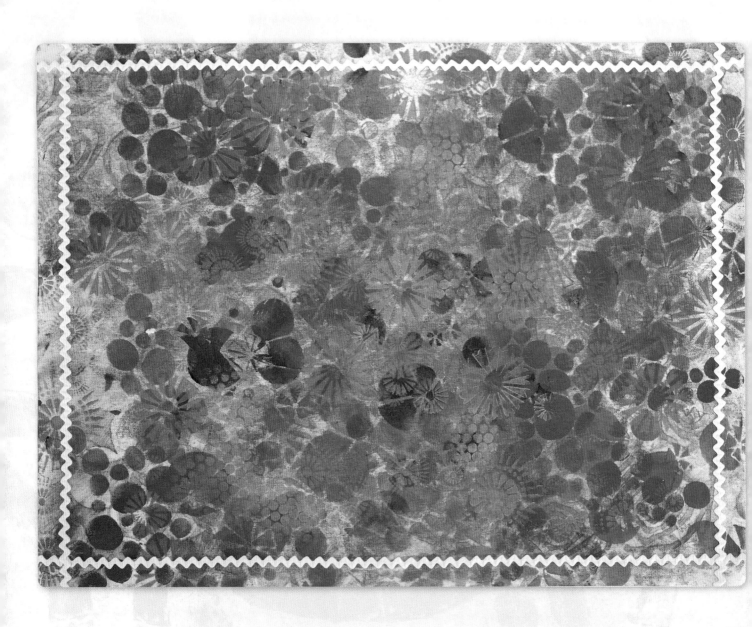

Sign up for our free newsletter at **www.CreateMixedMedia.com.**

# Improv Place Mat

**S**tencils may be used to create fabrics that will then lend themselves to tons of different household items. For this project, we are going to make a place mat, but you could just as easily make matching napkins, a tablecloth, tea towels, curtains or pillow shams.

Making fabric is gratifying because it allows me to truly personalize the decor of my house. I can pick precisely the colors I want to use and even use latex wall paint if I am trying to match a wall color. Using stencils makes it so easy because I am not limited to my drawing or painting ability. I can even convey a mood through my stencil choices. After you start making décor items, you will find it is so fun and reasonably priced that you will want to change things out with the seasons or with holidays. My favorite thing to do is to simply layer with abandon! It is an instantaneous way to establish depth within your hand-painted fabric.

## WHAT YOU NEED

- *Roc-lon Multi-Purpose Cloth*
- *rotary cutter or scissors*
- *cutting mat*
- *ruler*
- *stencils*
- *Gelli plate*
- *acrylic paints*
- *foam brush*
- *brayer*
- *spray bottle of water*
- *fabric glue*
- *rickrack or other trim*
- *polyurethane spray (optional)*

## Here's a Tip

For me, the discovery of Roc-lon cloth pretty much rocked my world because I am a very marginal seamstress. The opportunity to use a fabric that requires no prepping and no special paint is ideal for my spontaneous personality. This fabric also has a very smooth finish and cuts without fraying (plus it is quite durable). That being said, it is not machine washable, so you can only do spot cleaning. It has a somewhat rigid feel and would make great bookmarks, window shades or any type of item where you want it to hold its shape.

1 Cut your fabric down to size. A standard place mat is 14" x 18" (36cm x 46cm).

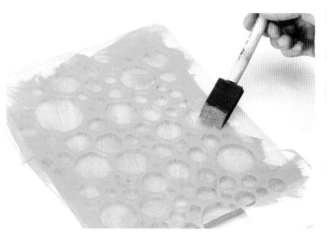

2 Choose your desired stencil, lay it on the Gelli plate and use a foam brush to spread bright blue acrylic paint over the stencil.

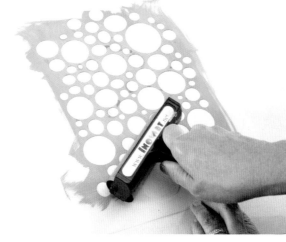

3 Press the wet side of the stencil on the place mat and use a brayer to apply pressure over the stencil. (My stencil already had dried blue paint on both sides.)

4 Spritz the stencil with water and repeat printing until you run out of paint and the mat is pretty well covered.

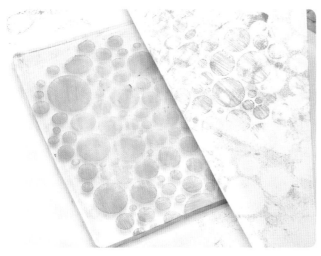

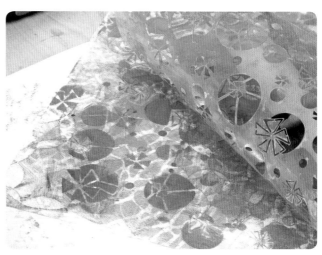

5 Go back to the Gelli plate, put your fabric face down and roll over it with a brayer or press gently with your hands. Spritz the Gelli plate with water and repeat. Keep repeating until you are out of paint.

6 Select another stencil and repeat steps 2 through 5 as desired until you decide your place mat is finished.

7 Create some depth by stenciling on a final layer of a contrasting color such as white.

8 Clean up the edges of the fabric if necessary with a rotary cutter. Run a bead of glue around the edges of the place mat, about ¾" (2mm) from the outside. Adhere rickrack to the glue. Note: If you want to make the place mat waterproof, spray it with polyurethane.

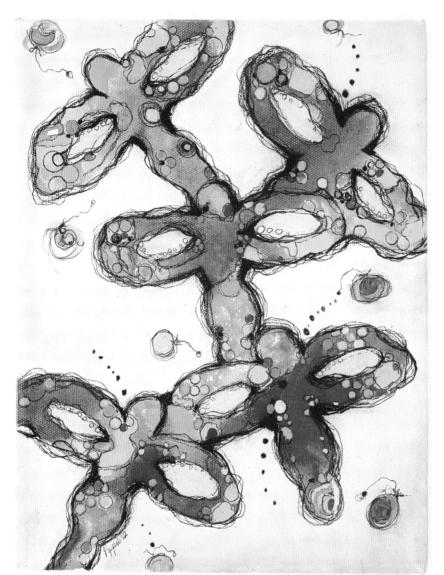

### *Dancing Dragonflies* by Pippin

Pippin started out by dripping and splattering warm-colored paint on a canvas. She then drew a dragonfly on paper and made a stencil by folding the paper in half and cutting it out. She placed the dragonfly stencil and outlined it, then used a commercial circle stencil for the small circles. Finally, she painted the background in white and used a fine black pen to outline the shapes.

### Bonus Project

After seeing Pippin's piece, I knew I wanted to see if I could save a couple of "failed" paintings using the same techniques.

You can see step-by-step instruction for this project at www.CreateMixedMedia. com/stencilgirl.

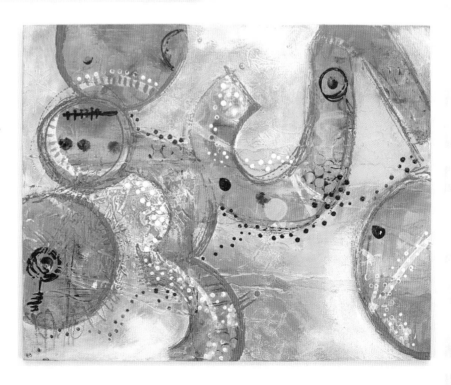

# Hands on the Wall Wallpaper

Handmade wallpaper is oh-so-trés chic, and I imagine this is how celebrities must certainly decorate their homes, don't you? I often watch decorator TV shows and see high-end decorators using such products. The price is just crazy expensive, so it's a good thing we are artists and can figure out how to do it ourselves.

One of the reasons I wanted to tackle this project was because of the texture. I have always wanted to abstractly texturize a few walls in my house, but I worried about the future. I mean, what happens when down the road I want to change my décor? I imagine a time-consuming situation of sanding all the texture off the wall. So why not make a textured design on a roll of kraft paper and simply wallpaper it to your wall? Yeah, I know it is a lot of work, but this would be fabulous on an entry wall or in a powder room—kind of a focal point.

If you aren't up for making wallpaper, you can certainly apply these same techniques directly to the wall (with or without the texture) or even to your art. Repeatable stencils applied directly to the wall will create a wallpaper look. There are loads of stencils on the market to accent any décor.

## WHAT YOU NEED

- *6ft (2m) tables, 2*
- *roll of kraft paper*
- *artist removable tape*
- *pencil*
- *stencils*
- *Wood Icing*
- *palette knife*
- *acrylic paint, analogous colors*
- *stencil brush or foam brush*
- *fluid acrylic paint, Micaceous Iron Oxide (Golden)*
- *paper towels*
- *metallic paint*
- *scissors*
- *wallpaper paste*

**1** To set up your space, put two long tables—6ft (2m) or so—end to end. (For photo purposes, here we are working smaller.) Unroll your kraft paper and place on the table. Tape to secure, using an artist tape that will not tear paper. Use a pencil to make registration marks. This will allow you to match up the stencil when you move it.

**2** Place some Wood Icing in random areas to add some texture. For this stencil, I alternated rows of the pattern. (Note: Discard excess icing that you scrape away in the trash, rather than down the drain, because it could plug up pipes.)

## Here's a Tip

Remove icing that accidentally got outside the intended stenciled areas before it dries, if you can. If you find dried texture product on the stencil itself, it can usually be removed by gently sanding the stencil with sandpaper. You can also soak the stencil in warm water and sometimes the texture will come right off.

**3** Keeping the stencil in place, add a layer of paint.

**4** Flip the stencil over and add more texture if desired.

**5** Now, again, keeping the stencil in place, paint with an analogous color to continue stenciling.

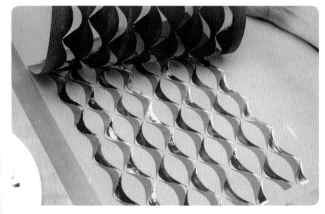

**6** Remove the stencil.

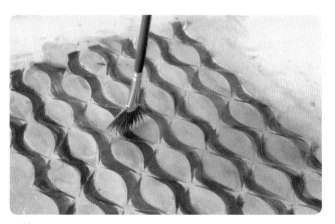

**7** Continue to paint using a third analogous color that you've mixed with Micaceous Iron Oxide. Blot up any excess paint with a paper towel. Reapply the stencil to touch up any areas that need defining. (This is where the registration marks are very helpful.) Drybrush over the textured parts using a metallic paint. When you're finished, trim the edges and apply to your wall with wallpaper paste.

### *Emperor's Door* by Rose Wilde

Another terrific home décor project is to stencil on cabinetry like Rose has done here. She used a three-layer stencil to create this art, which also required registration marks in order to keep the design intact. The texture used is Wood Icing and the paint is Annie Sloan Chalk Paint.

# STENCIL FUN

*Once you've mastered the wide variety of ways you can use stencils, you will quickly realize there are a ton of applications that cross over into other areas of your life. I am especially excited about the idea of personalizing some of my clothing. Not being a seamstress per se, I have always longed for ways to alter clothing with a method that was easily accessible. I am thrilled to know that stencils make this possible.*

I continue to come up with ideas that we haven't included here—fabric bracelets, doodled and stenciled shoes, purses, you name it! I know you are going to be just like me and will think of all kinds of new and fun options with your stencil collection. Keep me informed—a girl's gotta know!

Stencil on, my friends!

# Painted Memories Travel Journal

I am not what you would call a typical art journaler, but when traveling, I do enjoy keeping mementos of my trip—ticket stubs, found ephemera, etc. I like to document just enough so I can flip through the journal and summon up memories when I am back home. Here we will make a small journal—the exact one I make and use during my trips.

You will learn that painting and mark making do not always have to be done with traditional manufactured stencils. For this project, I have used a scrapbook template that has turned into one of my very favorite "stencils" that I use all the time. Although its manufactured use is not intended as a stencil, I like how it creates little boxes that turn into writing spaces within the journal.

I will also show you how to use objects that you find on your trip. Some can be adapted as makeshift stencils, and others will serve as collage elements for your journal.

## Here's a Tip

Matte paints are important for this project because they will give "tooth" to your paper, allowing you to easily write in your journal. Many craft-grade paints tend to dry down to a matte finish. If you are unable to find matte paint, you can use colored gessoes, or you can spray your pages with clear gesso.

## WHAT YOU NEED

- *140-lb. (300gsm) hot-pressed watercolor paper, half of a large sheet*
- *spray bottle of water*
- *stencils or scrapbook layout template*
- *matte-finish acrylic paints*
- *paintbrushes*
- *metal ruler*
- *pencil*
- *bone folder*
- *awl*
- *waxed linen thread/needle*
- *scissors*
- *collage materials*
- *cosmetic sponge*
- *rubbing wax*
- *light-weight paper*
- *ephemera from a favorite trip*
- *collage medium (such as Pam Carriker's Mixed Media Adhesive)*
- *Derwent Inktense pencils*

*1* Spritz your paper lightly on both sides so it is damp. Place a scrapbook template over the paper and paint with a few analogous colors.

*2* Remove the template.

**3** Spray the wet paint and hold the paper up vertically to allow the paint to drip and run on the paper. (You could also fold the paper over for an inkblot effect.)

**4** Repeat steps 2 and 3 until the paper is covered as desired. Allow to dry. Repeat the painting process on the other side of the paper and allow that side to dry.

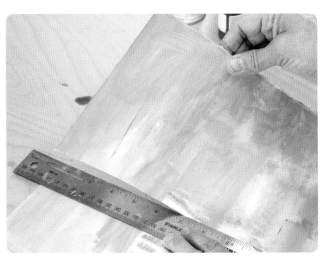

**5** Divide the short end of the paper into three sections using a ruler.

**6** Line up your metal ruler along the markings. Score with a bone folder. Fold the paper and score along the fold again. Tear the paper with the metal ruler.

**7** Fold each paper in half, and stack them together to create a signature, keeping in mind which sheet you want on the outside for the cover.

**8** Open to the center and mark three holes along the fold line where you will sew it together.

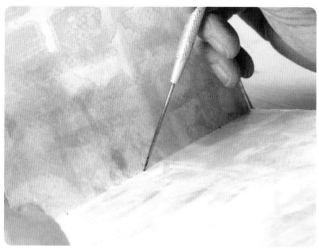

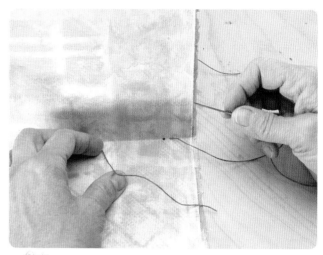

9  Use an awl to make a hole at each mark. You can use a binder clip to secure your pages together if you like. Be sure and poke through all the pages.

10  Cut a piece of waxed linen thread three times the length of the fold line. Thread the needle, but don't tie a knot. Leaving a tail of about 4" (10cm), sew from the center hole to the outside, then back in through one hole at one end.

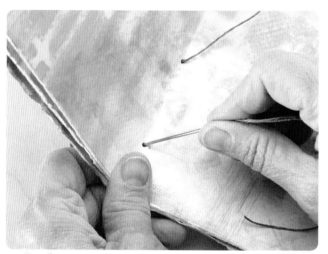

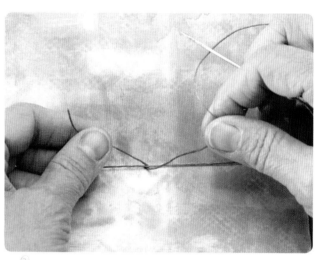

11  Skip the center hole and sew back from the inside hole at the opposite end to the outside.

12  Sew back through the center hole from the outside to the inside. Tie a knot.

13  Create a stencil out of found objects from your trip. In this case, I cut a wave from a page in a French magazine I found on my trip to Paris.

14  Using a cosmetic sponge, dab with an acrylic paint blend around your stencil on your journal page.

**15** Using rubbing wax, create a rubbing on a piece of paper that's covering a stencil.

**16** Start adding collage elements from your trip or bits that remind you of your trip. Use collage medium to adhere your collage elements to the page.

**17** Frame some of your collaged objects with additional stenciling.

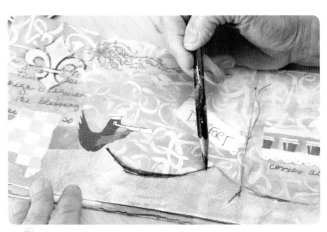

**18** Touch up areas of your page with Inktense pencils to add shadows or depth.

## Here's a Tip

Make rubbings while you're still on your trip. Things like a manhole cover that has a city name on it, plaques outside doors, interesting keyholes, gravestones—basically anything with texture makes a great rubbing and reminder of your trip.

Hard rubbing wax is excellent for rubbings, but many other things will work as well. Consider a hunk of encaustic paint or a simple crayon. Look in the children's section of any craft store and you will find great big crayons, sometimes even in a round shape. When rubbing, hold the wax at an angle to the object you are rubbing. This will give you a better result with a more crisp line.

## Here's a Tip

I don't like to carry a bunch of art supplies when I travel. I always make my journal ahead of time so I can minimize what I carry. My typical travel kit includes: glue stick, scissors, set of Inktense pencils, cosmetic sponge, one brush (Aqua Brush is good), rubbing wax and writing pen. I like the Sakura IDenti-pen, which has two tips and will write on anything.

**Sampler Book #1 by Andrew Borloz**

Front and Back Covers

Printed on a copy of an old page from *Harper's Bazaar* with a side cut from a plastic laundry basket (holes).

## Spread One

Hand-cut letter stencil (from hand-drawn letters) on an old page
from *Harper's Bazaar* and red-lined with a brayer.

## Spread Two

Color copy of art with spray paints and two stencils.

## Spread Three

Color copy of art with spray paints. Black image done with direct spraying through a stencil and a red image printed (with masking tape) with the stencil spray-painted first, then turned over and printed onto the paper.

### Spread Four

Color copy of dots stenciled with black spray paint, brayer-printed with white gesso and printed with a packaging foam piece.

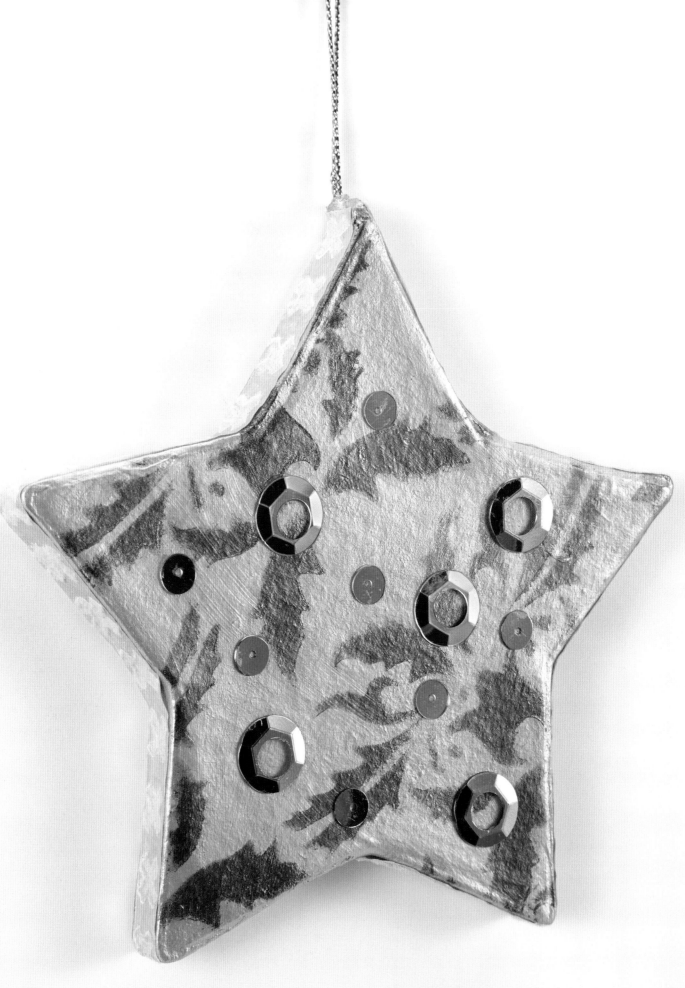

# All That Glitters

Stencils can pull off a fancy schmancy look when they are used with the right products. I'm talking about metallic paints, glitter and other embellishments that can enhance and adorn all of your artistic projects. There are so many of these things on the market now—mica, crushed glass, fake grass, fake snow, dimensional paints, felt, flocking, gold leaf and spray products. Also check out a model railroad hobby store for things such as fake wood by the sheet or fake bricks, and simply cut or glue the item into whatever shape you desire.

A papier mâché substrate is perfect for this type of project. I have chosen an ornament, but you could just as easily pick a large letter, a frame or one of the myriad options available at your craft store. This project is quick and easy, not to mention inexpensive!

## WHAT YOU NEED

- *papier mâché ornament or other object*
- *acrylic paint, metallic*
- *paintbrushes*
- *deli wrap*
- *stencil*
- *gold gesso*
- *Inka Gold*
- *transfer adhesive (Martha Stewart Crafts)*
- *flocking sheet (Martha Stewart Crafts)*
- *craft glue*
- *bone folder*
- *double-sided tape*
- *ruler*
- *craft knife*
- *sequins*

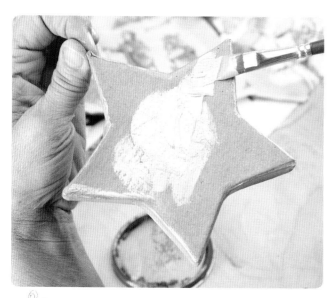

1. Paint a papier mâché star with a couple layers of metallic gold gesso.

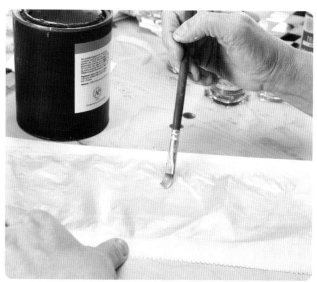

2. While your star is drying, paint a page of deli wrap or plain paper with gold gesso. This will be the start of your stenciled, decorative tape. Set the paper aside to dry.

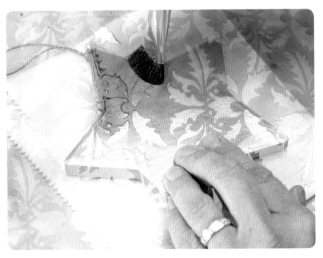

3 After the gold paint on the star is dry, place your selected stencil and paint Inka Gold (I used the Hematite color) over the star. Set aside to dry.

4 Going back to your gessoed deli wrap, place a stencil over the dried paint, and paint a layer of Martha Stewart's transfer adhesive (or any sort of glue that will hold glitter). Let it dry for about ten minutes.

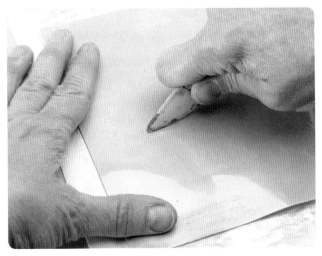

5 Set a sheet of flocking face down on the tacky stenciled area and burnish well with a bone folder or your fingers.

6 Peel back the piece of flocking.

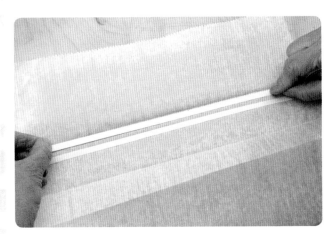

7 Create a fold along your flocked paper where you want your tape to be. Flip the paper over and adhere a piece of double-sided tape along the fold line. Fold the paper again for your next tape line and add another line of tape on the back. Repeat until you have several strips of tape.

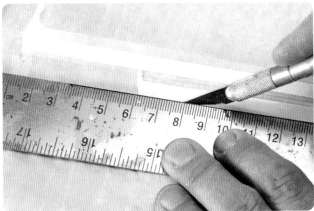

8 Using a ruler and a craft knife, cut along each side of the tape to create strips.

 Adhere the strips of tape along the edges of your star.

 Check to see if the Inka Gold is dry and if so, buff the stenciled areas to a shine.

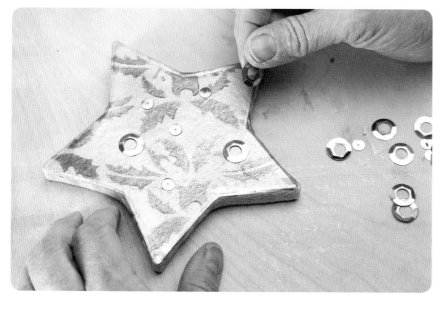

 Adhere some matching sequins as desired using craft or jeweler's glue.

### Stencil Holiday Gift Tags by Tracie Lyn Huskamp

Tracie used spray adhesive to apply glue to a medium shipping tag and then covered the tag with wrapping paper. After trimming the excess, she used her own design stencils (at StencilGirl Products) to trace designs of a songbird, swallow and rabbit onto watercolor paper. She cut out the animal shapes and sprayed them with adhesive, then covered the adhesive with glitter. She also sprayed the shapes with aerosol hairspray to lock the glitter into place. Finally, she attached the glitter critters to the tags with double-sided tape.

### Faux Metal Box Bonus Project

To make this faux metal box, I created texture on a papier mâché box in several different ways. On the sides, I used a texture medium (Wood Icing), and on the top, I used pieces of pasta. I experimented with several metal-type products, including aluminum foil, to achieve the effect.

You can see step-by-step instruction for this project at www.CreateMixedMedia.com/stencilgirl.

Sign up for our free newsletter at www.**CreateMixedMedia**.com.

# Eat Cake

My friend Deb is a pastry chef. She makes amazing things that are both beautiful and edible. There is no such thing as an ordinary cake in her book. Frankly, I never knew that stencils were even used in the pastry biz until she mentioned it to me. And that is when I knew I had to try it!

If you are also new to this world, just walk down the cake-decorating aisle at your local craft store. It is unreal how many of the supplies are similar to, if not the same as, supplies used in the mixed-media world. Fondant is an icing, yet it rolls out much like clay, and this basically serves as your substrate for decorating. Beyond that you can find spreadable icing (precolored just like paint!) and spray icings that work like airbrushes. There is even icing in "writer tip" containers just like my beloved Scribbles. Yep, edible dimensionals.

Make sure all of your supplies for decorating cupcakes or cakes with stencils are used only for food. Do not use the same stencils for edible food as you would use for painting.

## WHAT YOU NEED

- *store-bought fondant*
- *wax paper*
- *powdered sugar*
- *rolling pin*
- *cookie cutter or craft knife*
- *stencils (dedicated to food use)*
- *icing*
- *palette knife (for food use)*
- *cupcake or cake that needs to be iced*
- *optional: sprinkles, icing spray mist, icing with writing tips*

## FROSTING OVER FONDANT

Just as you can apply Wood Icing over a stencil, so can you use a stencil to apply cake frosting over fondant.

1. Knead the fondant until it is malleable.

2. Sprinkle powdered sugar on the wax paper and roll the fondant to the desired thickness.

**3** Use a cookie or biscuit cutter to cut the fondant in a cute round shape.

**4** Lay your selected stencil on the cut fondant, and using a clean palette knife, spread icing over the stencil.

**5** Remove your stencil to reveal your design.

**6** Add any other designs you like using icing decorator tips.

**7** Add a thin layer of icing to the top of the cupcake. This will be the "glue" that will keep the fondant in place.

**8** Place the fondant on top of the cupcake and gently press down the edges.

## MIST SPRAY OVER FONDANT

Think layering here. Just as you might layer sheer fluids or airbrush paints, use stencils to mist with a decorating spray. You could also decorate your cupcake in another way, then spray around the edges only. These sprays are quite sheer and are the most visible over white icing or fondant.

Instead of painting a stencil with icing, you could spray the stencil using Color Mist cake-decorating spray (like an airbrush). If you've chosen a colored fondant, add a bit of white icing to the top to allow the Color Mist to show through.

## FONDANT SHAPES OVER FONDANT

A stencil can be your guide for cutting out fondant when shapes you might want are not available in cookie-cutter form.

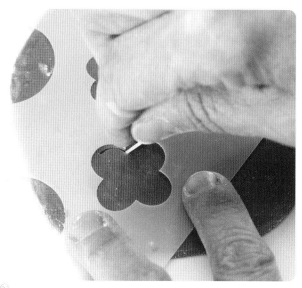

1 Roll out a piece of fondant and use a stencil to cut out a shape with a clean, sharp knife such as a craft knife (wet the blade with hot water to allow for smooth cutting).

2 Add a little icing on top, then adhere sprinkles. Once again, use icing to adhere the fondant pieces to the fondant on top of your cupcake.

Sign up for our free newsletter at **www.CreateMixedMedia.com.**

# T-ease Me

I have already confessed that I am not much of a seamstress; however, I do enjoy hand-sewing. Natalie (Alabama) Chanin inspired this project. Of course, I don't really know her, but I worship the clothes that her company makes. The moment I saw their designs, I was immediately in awe and instantly knew I must try it for myself. I had never heard of reverse appliqué before, but, I figured out how to do it because anything involving stencils and clothes is for me!

Flip through the clothing in your closet and I feel certain you will find a T-shirt that you love but never wear because it has a stain or a tiny hole. That is the perfect shirt for this project. Alternatively, you can purchase a shirt at a discount or thrift store. Also locate some coordinating T-shirt material (or paint it yourself!) to use for the appliqués and you are ready to go.

## WHAT YOU NEED

- *T-shirt and fabric scraps*
- *cutting mat*
- *stencil*
- *pencil*
- *sewing pins*
- *sewing needle and thread*
- *scissors*

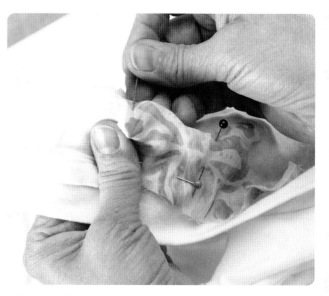

1 Collect the fabrics and T-shirts that you want to use. It is best to stick with all prewashed jersey. Place your T-shirt on a stable surface and trace a light pencil outline around the area you want to cut out. You may or may not find it easier to put a piece of cardboard inside your shirt to keep it flat.

2 Carefully pin your selected fabric scrap behind the traced area (right side of the scrap facing the wrong side of the T-shirt), taking care that the fabric will cover your entire stencil area.

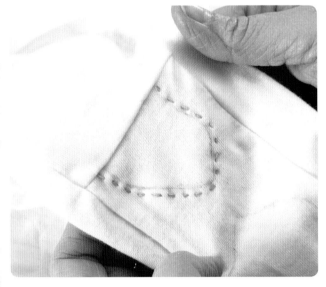

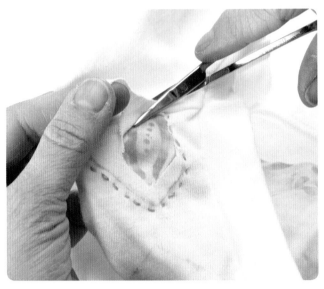

3 Start hand-stitching along the outside of your pencil line. Make sure your underneath cloth is flat and you are stitching through both layers.

4 Using well-sharpened scissors, very carefully cut inside your stitched line to reveal the fabric underneath.

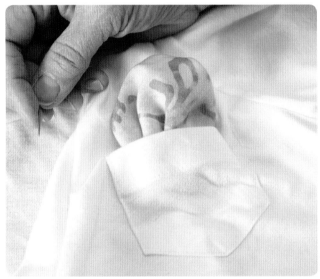

5 Repeat steps 2 through 4 for other shapes on the shirt.

6 If your shirt has a pocket, tuck a piece of fabric in there and sew it from the inside of the shirt.

## Here's a Tip

You can vary this project in tons of different ways. You could add beading. Or add appliqué on top of the T-shirt. Consider using a more intricate stitch. Use tone on tone or pattern on pattern; vary it up. I have started saving all of my "old" T-shirts and have plans for every single one of them. I have this crazy urge to personalize nearly every garment I own, so trust me when I say this could be slightly addictive.

### *Stencil Hair Ponies* by June Pfaff Daley

Start with cotton fabric, printed or plain. Positioning the stencil on the fabric, use fabric markers (June uses Tee Juice by Jaquard) to fill in the desired part of the stencil. Iron a piece of Craft-Fuse to the back of the project. Cut out the fused shape, leaving a little extra room around the edges. Hand-stitch or machine-sew in different colored threads to enhance the design. Embellish with seed beads as desired. Cut a piece of wool felt the same size as the front. Pin the pieces together. Using a sewing machine, zigzag stitch the edges of the two pieces together. Finish by hand-stitching a hair pony to the back center of the piece.

Sign up for our free newsletter at **www.CreateMixedMedia.com**.

# Greetings, Greetings, Greetings

**M**y introduction to the art world was in 1992 when I started making greeting cards. I had meandered into a rubber stamp store (thinking it was a stationery shop because I needed to buy invitations), and the proprietor, Kristin Powers, showed me the ropes. I was hooked, and from 1992 until 1998, I made every single greeting card that I sent. I'm not sure what happened after that time, but I recently realized how much I miss making greeting cards. They are so satisfying to make—a project that can be finished in a short amount of time. Ya gotta love it.

In this project, I introduce a few new ways to use stencils when making greeting cards. You can also apply these techniques to other mixed-media projects. And after we warm up with a couple of cards, I will share my tips on how you can cut your own stencils.

## Here's a Tip

I find the scratching process to be quite soothing (probably due to its brainless quality). I use a clipboard so I can easily hold the project on my lap and scratch while watching TV or even riding in a car. I accumulate a lot of elements to add to my stash by working this way.

## BLACK SCRATCH PAPER

You may be familiar with scratch board, but did you know you can buy scratch paper that offers the same fun scratching process?

## WHAT YOU NEED

- *black scratch paper*
- *stencils*
- *clipboard (optional)*
- *craft knife or dental tool*
- *PITT Artist Big Brush Pens in assorted colors*
- *cardstock or premade cards*
- *watercolor paints/acrylic paints and brushes*
- *foam brushes*
- *ruler*
- *double-sided tape*
- *frisket*
- *Scribbles Dimensional FabricPaint*
- *eraser*
- *stencil film or Mylar*
- *lightbox*
- *source photo*
- *permanent marker*
- *tape*
- *ceramic tile or piece of glass*
- *stencil cutting tool*
- *piece of paper*
- *Radiant Rain Shimmering Mist*

**1** Cut a piece of black scratch paper down to the size you want to be the centerpiece of your card. (I've chosen 4" [10cm] square.) Clip the paper and the stencil together with a clipboard. If you don't have a clipboard, tape the stencil into place. Using a sharp object (craft knife, dental tool, scribe, etc.), scratch the paper in the open areas of the stencil to reveal the white.

**2** You may wish to use more than one stencil, like I did. When you are finished scratching, remove the paper from the clipboard and lift off the stencil.

3 Using PITT Artist Big Brush Pens, color in the white parts created by the scratching.

4 Switching to the blank card, paint a stenciled background on the front of the card using acrylic paint and a foam brush. Match up the stencil edge to edge as you fill the front of the card.

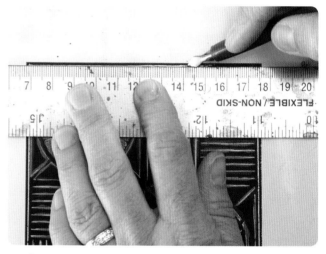

5 Add a bit of the paint used on the card to the scratched design to connect the two pieces.

6 You may choose to scratch a few more white spaces in the background to create a border.

7 Apply double-sided tape to the back of the scratch paper.

8 Mount the scratch paper to the card.

## FRISKET AND WATERCOLOR PAPER

Frisket acts as a resist, and there are many ways to use it. Using a stencil as a guide, it's fun to create added details such as these little dots.

1 Using the end of a paintbrush (or an embossing tool), apply dots of frisket through a stencil to a piece of paper. (The frisket dots will preserve white space when you add watercolor.)

2 When the frisket is dry, replace the stencil and paint with watercolor over the top.

3 If the stencil design allows, rotate it and paint over the stencil with watercolor again—using a different color. Allow the paper to dry.

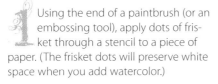

4 Add additional watercolor paint as a background around the stenciled image.

5 If you desire, outline your stenciled image with dimensional paint to emphasize the design.

6 Using an eraser, rub off the frisket, revealing the spots.

7 Adhere the paper to the card using double-sided tape.

## DOUBLE-LAYER STENCIL

You can achieve even greater interest and depth when you use a stencil that has different layers for different parts of the complete image.

### Here's a Tip

While it might seem easy enough to do the actual cutting to make a stencil, it is the drawing of the design that can be tricky because there is the issue of "islands" and "bridges," meaning the parts that are cut away versus the parts that hold the stencil together. My best advice is to take it slow and practice. You will eventually get "the eye" and be able to see/decide where to cut and not to cut.

**1** Cut two pieces of stencil film (or Mylar) to the same size. (Taping them together makes it easier.) Make sure your source image will fit on the pieces.

**2** Using a lightbox, lay the Mylar over the source photo (in this case, one of my paintings). Using a permanent marker, make registration marks on the four corners of the photo and make the same dots on the film along with an "up" arrow.

**3** Start to trace the first layer of the stencil (you won't trace the whole image for this first stencil, just select parts).

**4** Keeping the first piece of film in place, add the second piece of film on top and tape in place. Add the same registration marks and trace the part of the source photo that you didn't capture on the first piece of film.

**5** Tape the first piece of Mylar to a surface that will not burn, such as a smooth ceramic tile or a piece of glass (edges taped off with duct tape). Using an electric stencil cutting tool, follow your lines and cut out the "islands." The areas that are not cut are called "bridges."

**6** Repeat with the second sheet of stencil film. (If smaller pieces of the film won't fall out easily, poke them out using an awl or needle tool.)

## Here's a Tip

Many different kinds of stencil film are on the market, and I think I have tried all of them. Some of the materials are too thick and very difficult to cut. Some of them bead up along the edge when burned with a hot tool. The film that I use consistently with complete success is called E-Z Cut Stencil Material and is available from pjstencils.com. I prefer the 6mm although you may want the 10mm if you wish to work big. It honestly does cut like butter as they claim!

**7** Stencil the bottom (first) stencil onto the card using your chosen color of acrylic paint.

**8** Remove the first stencil. Add the second stencil and second color of paint. Remove the stencil.

**9** Mask the area you just stenciled with a piece of paper. Place a stencil for the background over the mask and card, and spray Radiant Rain Shimmering Mist (or mist color of your choice) over the entire card.

**10** Remove your stencil and mask. If you want, choose another stencil to layer with another color.

# CONTRIBUTORS

### Wendy Aikin

After a successful career in finance, a ten-year stint with a nonprofit and sending three great kids off to college, Wendy and her husband, Roger, moved to Italy. For Roger it was a job with NATO and for Wendy it was like falling into a rabbit hole. An art-class junkie (assemblage, book binding and papermaking) turned loose in the art capital of the world was a dangerous thing. After three years of trolling galleries and museums, she moved back home and dove into drawing, painting and clay classes. At an open studio, Wendy discovered her first encaustic painting, and it was love at first sight. Of course, more classes were needed and, eventually, training at R&F Handmade Paints in Kingston, New York (the premier encaustic paintmakers in the United States).

Wendy can most often be found putting together junk (assemblage), tearing up paper and pasting it to stuff (collage) or pursuing her passion: painting with hot wax (encaustic) in the studio she shares with her sister Judy Stabile. In her spare time, Wendy teaches encaustic painting along with her business partners, Judy Stabile and Daniella Woolf, at Wax Works West studio in Corralitos, California.
www.wendyaikin.com
www.waxworkswest.com

### Margaret Applin

Margaret is a mixed-media artist living in Lowell, Massachusetts. Born and raised in New England, Margaret's art is full of inspiration taken from the natural landscape and the changing seasons. With a solid commitment to creating personal imagery, Margaret explores various techniques to develop the building blocks that define her artwork. Margaret has been published in *Quilting Arts, Somerset Studio Gallery* and *Art Doll Quarterly* magazines. She has also completed a Quilting Arts Workshop DVD titled *Digital Design for Screen Printing*, and is currently working on her second DVD through *Cloth Paper Scissors* magazine. Margaret sells her digital designs as Thermofax screens on her Etsy site and is currently developing stencil designs.
www.scrapwisdomcollage.blogspot.com
www.margaretapplindesigns.com
www.etsy.com/shop/free2design

### Seth Apter

Seth is a mixed-media artist, author and instructor from New York City. His artwork has been exhibited in numerous exhibitions throughout the United States and Canada, and can be found in multiple books, independent zines and national magazines. Seth is the voice behind *The Pulse*, a series of international, collaborative projects that are the basis of his book *The Pulse of Mixed Media: Secrets and Passions of 100 Artists Revealed* (North Light Books). He is also the artist behind two workshop DVDs by North Light Media: *Easy Mixed Media Surface Techniques* and *Easy Mixed Media Techniques for the Art Journal*. Seth is currently working on his second North Light book, *The Mixed Media Artist*, to be released in October 2013.
www.thealteredpage.blogspot.com

### Andrew Borloz

Ever since Andrew Borloz was a kid, he has been exploring and hunting for color, texture and design wherever he goes. After his training in industrial design at the University of Bridgeport in Connecticut, in computer science at Montclair State College in New Jersey and in book arts and printing at the Center for Book Arts in New York City, he has developed a personal lifetime collection of creative works in various creative disciplines such as fine art, origami, mixed media, exhibit design, product design, book arts, letterpress printing and printmaking. Andrew is currently self-employed as an artist/designer/instructor.

### Pam Carriker

Pam is a mixed-media artist, instructor and author of the book, *Art at the Speed of Life* (Interweave Press). Her articles and artwork can be found in more than forty publications including *Somerset Studio* (cover artist Nov/Dec 2010), *The Stampers' Sampler, Art Journaling* (cover artist Summer 2010), *Somerset Apprentice, Where Women Create, Artful Blogging, Cloth Paper Scissors* and *Studios*. Serving as a Directors' Circle artist for Stampington & Company, Pam has also created instructional videos for Strathmore Artist Papers' line of Visual Journals, stencils for *StencilGirl* Products and rubber art stamps for Stampington & Company. She is enjoying developing a signature line of mixed-media art products with Matisse Derivan, and her next book is due out in Fall 2013 (Interweave Press). www.pamcarriker.com

### Lisa Cousineau

Lisa is the girl half of Artistcellar.com, a little piece of the Web that provides a variety of unique and high-quality stencils and art supplies to mixed-media artists, art journalers and textile artists. When she is not getting paint all over herself, she can be found taking photographs, reading or hanging out with her husband, Michael, the other half of Artistcellar, and her daughter, Celia, chief product tester. www.artistcellar.com www.facebook.com/artistcellar

# CONTRIBUTORS

### Jen Cushman

Jen is a natural storyteller who found mixed-media art a decade ago and never looked back. She's drawn to the imperfect, the quirky, the artsy and the authentic—be it people, objects or art. Jen's jewelry, collage and assemblage has been featured in *Belle Armoire Jewelry*, *Somerset Studio*, *Somerset Life*, *Mingle*, *Cloth Paper Scissors*, *Wirework* and *Jewelry Affaire* magazines, as well as on the websites of Mary Engelbreit's Home Companion and on the Crafts Channel of Lifetime Television. Currently the director of education and marketing for ICE Resin, Jen is also a Designer Member of the Craft & Hobby Association (CHA) and won an award for "Most Innovative Design" at the Winter CHA 2011 show. She is the author of two books: *Making Metal Jewelry: How to Stamp, Forge, Form and Fold Metal Jewelry Designs* (North Light Books) and self-published *Explore, Create, Resinate: Mixed Media Techniques Using ICE Resin*. She also writes a marketing advice column for *Belle Armoire Jewelry* called "Art Chooses You" and is a contributing editor for Create Mixed Media. www.jencushman.com

### Tracie Lyn Huskamp

Tracie shares her love of art and nature through the release of her book, *Nature Inspired* (Quarry Publishing), and by teaching workshops at some of the most prestigious national and international retreats and conferences. Her mixed-media work has received national recognition. Tracie has appeared on ABCNews.com, in an Associated Press interview, on the cover of *Somerset Studio* magazine and in feature articles in various other publications. She has contributed her art and designs to more than ten books. Tracie is also pursuing the dream of licensing artwork with three fabric collections by Windham Fabrics, three calendar collections by TF Publishing and several scrapbooking and art products. www.TheRedDoor-Studio.com

### Jane LaFazio

Jane has been a full-time artist since 1998 and truly believes she is living the life she was meant to live! In that time, she has cultivated a wide range of skills as a painter, mixed-media/quilt artist, art teacher and blogger. Jane is known for her fun-loving, creative teaching style and providing a relaxed, supportive environment in the classroom. She teaches workshops online and at art retreats internationally. Jane's artwork has been featured in *Cloth Paper Scissors* and *Quilting Arts* magazines many times, in Danny Gregory's book *An Illustrated Life* and in numerous other books. Her instructional DVDs: *From Art Journaling to Art*, *Layered & Fused Appliqué Quilts: From Fabric Scraps to Recycled Circles* and *The Small Art Quilt* are available on Amazon. www.JaneLaFazio.com

### Leighanna Light

Leighanna is an art instructor and mixed-media assemblage artist. Her background is in fine arts and photography, and she has been teaching art workshops, locally and internationally for the past fifteen years. Leighanna is represented by galleries and museums across the country, and her work has been published in numerous books and magazines. Leighanna grew up in a small town in upstate New York and has spent most of the past twenty years in New Mexico. She currently resides in Taos, New Mexico, with her best friends, Thomas and Sam.

www.lklight.blogspot.com
www.thingmakerstudio.blogspot.com
www.lklight.etsy.com

### Laurie Mika

Laurie is an artist, author and instructor. Over the last two decades, her mixed-media mosaic work has evolved into an original and easily recognizable style. Laurie's unique approach combines handmade polymer clay tiles with beads, jewelry pieces, charms, glass tile and found objects. She feels very fortunate to be able to combine her love of travel and passion for art through teaching at art retreats. Laurie's work has been published in numerous magazines and included in more than a dozen books. She has appeared on both HGTV's *That's Clever* and on DIY's *Craft Lab*. Laurie's own book, *Mixed-Media Mosaics,* was published by North Light Books. Closer to home in southern California, Laurie participates in juried exhibitions and has her work in galleries and private collections.

www.mikaarts.com

### Mary C. Nasser

Mary is an artist and art educator living in the greater St. Louis area. Her art is inspired by nature—specifically, landscapes and geology. Mary loves creating mixed-media paintings layered with maps and geologic drawings. She is captivated by the idea that geological shifts and transformations seem to parallel both individuals and their relationships—continually changing, varying, shifting and developing, too.

www.marycnasser.com
www.facebook.com/marynasserart
www.twitter.com/marycnasser

### Carole Perry

Carole is a native of southern Oregon who now works out of her desert studio in Cave Creek, Arizona. A number of years ago, she set aside a successful career in computers to pursue her passion for glass full time. "I ran after the executive brass ring for twenty years before admitting it could never hold the same sparkle as the art glass I'd been collecting for almost as many years. My idols were Chihuly, Marquis and Brock, rather than Iacocca or Watson."
"While I enjoyed every day of those years with IBM and Xerox, nothing could prepare me for the sheer joy of creating a piece of glass sculpture. Finding my own way, without any set procedures, has felt like the equivalent of discovering the New World. Learning to live off my own feedback, with no measuring stick beyond my personal standards, has been the most rewarding experience of my life."
www.laughingglass.com

# CONTRIBUTORS

### June Pfaff Daley

June is a graphic designer and a mixed-media artist who creates with everything from wood to fabric. She enjoys transforming thrift store treasures and favors whimsical motifs. June resides in Cincinnati, Ohio, with three fantastic kids, one supportive husband, one charming cat and now a darling dog.
www.junepfaffdaley.com

### Pippin Schupbach

Pippin is a mixed-media artist living in St. Louis, Missouri. In her paintings, she likes to use intense color to convey her love of nature. Pippin also finds pleasure in the process of learning new ways to transmit joy through her art.
www.artpippin.blogspot.com
www.etsy.com/shop/artpippin

### Joanne Sharpe

"Whimsical art maker" Joanne is a colorful mixed-media artist and enthusiastic teacher with a passion for art journaling, lettering, doodling and illustration. Her playful art has been featured in *Cloth Paper Scissors*, *Studios*, *Somerset Studio*, *Somerset Art Journaling* and *Somerset Apprentice* magazines. In addition to teaching nationwide, Joanne has been licensing artwork to the craft, fabric and giftware markets for two decades. Joanne resides in Rochester, New York.

www.joannezsharpe.blogspot.com

### Lisa Sisley-Blinn

Lisa holds an MFA in printmaking from Western Michigan University, Gwen Frostic School of Art, where she is counted as one of the Alumni 100 for her work combining art and technology. During her graduate studies, she earned several awards and scholarships, studied waterless lithography at the University of Saskatchewan and was awarded a second scholarship to the Vermont Studio Center in Johnson, Vermont. While at Western Michigan University, Lisa taught Lithography on Aluminum Plate, Foundation Drawing and 2D Digital Imaging, as well as supervised both the undergraduate and graduate galleries. She has taught at the Kalamazoo Institute of Arts and the Battle Creek Art Institute in Michigan, and she continues to teach at the St. Louis Artists' Guild, St. Charles Community College and her private studio in O'Fallon, Missouri. In 2012 Lisa formed the St. Louis, Missouri artist group, WaxCentric. She is currently exploring the intersection of technology and fine art through painting, printmaking, photography and digital imaging. Lisa's recent work combines liminal spaces and the interplay of digital generative systems. Her work is held in private collections around the country.
www.sisleyblinn.wordpress.com
www.waxcentric.wordpress.com

### Julie Snidle

Once a corporate training administrator, Julie now works as a mixed-media artist specializing in encaustic work. With a degree in elementary education, she has taught art professionally in the classroom, juried artwork for the Mastodon Art/Science Fair and continues to teach workshops in the greater St. Louis area and around the United States. Largely self-taught in a variety of mixed-media techniques, Julie has studied encaustics intensively for nearly ten years, including specialized training with R&F Handmade Paints. Her art appears in *Printmaking + Mixed Media* by Dorit Elisha (Interweave Press) and *Flavor for Mixed Media* by Mary Beth Shaw (North Light). Julie is a member of the Encaustic Art Institute, WaxCentric and Art Saint Louis. Her work has appeared in juried shows around the Midwest and is in private and corporate collections nationwide. A native of Minneapolis, Julie resides in Festus, Missouri with her husband, Will.
www.juliesnidle.com

### Michelle Ward

Michelle is a mixed-media artist, freelance graphic designer and workshop instructor. She enjoys experimenting in different dimensional art forms but always returns to her favorite thing—working with paper and paint in journals. Michelle is a regular contributor to *Somerset Studio* magazine, and her work can be found in several books on journaling and related paper arts. She is a rubber stamp and stencil designer, operating Green Pepper Press from her home studio in New Jersey, where she lives with her husband and their three children.
www.greenpepperpress.com
www.michelleward.typepad.com

### Rose Wilde

Rose is the developer of Wood Icing, "The Great Cover Up," which is a resurfacing product used for furniture and cabinetry. For the last ten years, she has traveled around the country teaching her technique to decorative painters and has always had an online presence selling her product. When an opportunity to lease a space at the Chesterfield Mall in Chesterfield, Missouri, presented itself, Rose and her daughter, fine artist Heather Haymart, decided to come together as a team in one location. Heather manages the art gallery and Rose manages the Wood Icing retail area. Heather creates her beautiful paintings and Rose creates designs for furniture and cabinetry. They have realized the potential for becoming a resource for connecting people who would like to make a home or workspace beautiful by combining their individual passions into one inventive business.
www.woodicing.com

## RESOURCES

For a list of stenciling resources, visit www.CreateMixedMedia.com/stencilgirl.

# Index

Aikin, Wendy, 51, 118
All That Glitters, 96–99
applicators, 6
Applin, Margaret, 21, 32, 118
appliqué, reverse, 106
Apter, Seth, 27, 118

batik, 72–74
beeswax, 45, 73
bleach, 35
Borloz, Andrew, 93, 119
brushes, 6, 47
bubbles, 24, 48

cake decorating, 102–105
Can-Can Lantern, 56–58
cards, 110–117
Carriker, Pam, 17, 119
carving, 11
claybord, 11, 15
clothing, 106–108
collage, 24
color wheel, 67
Cousineau, Lisa, 28, 119
Cushman, Jen, 59, 120

Daley, June Pfaff, 109, 123
daubers, sponge, 6
depth, 13, 23, 42, 52, 79, 80
dimension, 39–43
doodles, 77

Eat Cake, 102–105
embellishments, 97
encaustic painting, 45–53, 92
etching technique, 59, 60, 61, 71

fabric, 79
Felt-A-Rama, 62–64
felting technique, 63–64
foam plates, 41
fondant, 102–105
found objects, 7
frisket, 113
frosting, cake, 102
fusing technique, 46–48

gel medium, 24, 35, 37
Gelli plate, 80
gesso, 35, 37, 88
Greetings, Greetings, Greetings, 110–117

hand sanitizer, 35
Hands on the Wall Wallpaper, 82–84
hole punching technique, 57–58
How Can You Resist a Fish?, 34–37
Huskamp, Tracie Lyn, 100, 121

icing. See Wood Icing
Improv Place Mat, 78–80
Inktense pencil, 14

journal, 88–92

LaFazio, Jane, 76, 120
lantern, 56–58
layering technique, 11, 21, 23, 67, 79, 105
Let's Get Dimensional, 38–42
Light, Leighanna, 60, 120

Magazine Magic, 30–32
masks, 5, 7, 23–26, 29
Mika, Laurie, 43, 121
mirror, 66–68
molding paste, 28

Nasser, Mary C., 16, 121
negative images, 41

paint, 37, 67, 88, 97
Painted Memories Travel Journal, 88–92
palette knife, 11
papier mâché, 97
Perry, Carole, 70, 121
place mats, 78–80
pop-up objects, 39

Quilt Me Batik, 72–74

removal process, 21, 33, 35
repetition, 11, 32
resists, 35–37, 51, 113
Ron-Ion cloth, 79
roving, 64
rubbings, 31, 92

sand paper, 31, 33
Schupbach, Pippin, 81, 123
scratching technique, 111
screens, 32
Sharpe, Joanne, 65, 123
shellac, 49
Sisley-Blinn, Lisa, 53, 122
Snidle, Julie, 52, 53, 122
Spray It Again, Sam, 66–68
stencils/stenciling
    art projects, 8–53
    cleaning, 12
    cutting, 115
    décor projects, 54–85
    double-layer, 115
    fun projects, 86–117
    hand-cut, 7
    materials, 116
    reverse (See masks)
    supplies, 6–7
    types of, 7
substrates, 7, 39, 97
supplies, 6–7

T-ease Me, 106–108
texture, 11, 12, 83, 101
Thermo-Fax, 32
Think-Outside-the-Stencil painting, 10–14
three-dimensional objects, 39–43
tooth, 88
travel kit, 92

Unmask That Paper Doll, 22–26
unryu paper, 73

wallpaper, 82–84
Ward, Michelle, 69, 123
wax, 35, 73, 92
Wax and Waning Encaustic, 44–49
Wilde, Rose, 85, 122
wipe-out technique, 69
wood-burning, 19–20
Wood Icing, 12, 39, 43, 83, 84, 101
Woulda Coulda Burn Wood, 18–20

Yupo paper, 58

## DEDICATION

I dedicate this book to my grandparents, who instilled in me an entrepreneurial spirit and confidence that has guided my life; they helped me believe I could succeed at absolutely anything.

## ACKNOWLEDGMENTS

As always, my husband, John, props me up and is the best life partner that a girl could ever imagine.

I give a special thanks to the entire staff at North Light who have been so kind and supportive to me; Tonia, you are simply the best.

And to my guest artists, your talent overwhelms me. Thank you for participating!

17  16  15  14  13    5  4  3  2  1

Distributed in Canada by Fraser Direct
100 Armstrong Avenue
Georgetown, ON, Canada  L7G 5S4
Tel: (905) 877-4411

Distributed in the U.K. and Europe by F&W Media International
Brunel House, Newton Abbot, Devon, TQ12 4PU, England
Tel: (+44) 1626 323200, Fax: (+44) 1626 323319
E-mail: enquiries@fwmedia.com

Distributed in Australia by Capricorn Link
P.O. Box 704, S. Windsor, NSW 2756 Australia
Tel: (02) 4577-3555

Editor: Tonia Jenny
Designer: Wendy Dunning
Photographer: Christine Polomsky
Production Coordinator: Greg Nock

# ABOUT MARY BETH

Mary Beth Shaw works in mixed media because she loves to play with art supplies. She uses stencils on anything and everything; if it will hold still, she will stencil it. Mary Beth's spontaneous process utilizes pastel, ink, marker and acrylics layered with various collage, texture and three-dimensional materials. She welcomes so-called "mistakes" because they lead to wonderful opportunities and discoveries. Mary Beth is author of *Flavor for Mixed Media* published by North Light Books, is a columnist for *Somerset Studio* magazine and is the owner of StencilGirl Products. Living in Wildwood, Missouri with her husband and three cats, Mary Beth is passionate about every moment of life.

   www.mbshaw.com
   www.mbshaw.blogspot.com
   www.stencilgirlproducts.com
   www.stencilgirlbook.com

PHOTO CREDIT: ©GREG BARTH PROJECTS, LLC